Human Bridges

Katherine De Lorraine

Plain View Press
P. O. 42255
Austin, TX 78704

plainviewpress.net
sb@plainviewpress.net
512-441-2452

Copyright Katherine De Lorraine 2009. All rights reserved.
ISBN: 978-0-911051-32-2
Library of Congress Number: 2009921666

Cover artwork from Africa Direct

Acknowledgements

Some of these poems have seen prior publication in the following journals: *Poet Lore, Negative Capability, The Hampden-Sydney Poetry Review, Appalachian Heritage, Correio das Artes, Green River Review, Virginia Writing*, and in the author's prize-winning chapbook *Someone You Should Know*, Armstrong State College, Savannah, GA.

Contents

Preface   7

Part 1: Women of Weya

Manena	11
Journey 1	12
Ngozi	13
Three Wives	14
Chimurenga	15
Eveline	16
Journey 2	17
Kutando Botso	18
Sheela	19
Chenura	20
Journey 3	21
Tima	22
Unmarried	23
Barika	24
Journey 4	25
Silent One Speaks	26
Ex-Combatant	27
Journey 5	28
Brother-In-Law	29
Karua's Dilemma	30
Motosai	31
Journey 6	32
Annie	33
Efo	34
Journey 7	35
Filis	36
Ella	37
Journey 8	38
Mr. Mudzingwa's Death	39
Brema	40
Journey 9	41
Uroyi	42
Gudza	43
Kufamaba Famba	44
Journey 10	45

Runyoka	46
Katesi	47
Journey 11	48

Part 2: Java and Jive

Supplication	51
Trying Not To Be Born	52
Confessing My Father	53
Trauma	54
Gray Barn	55
The Devil's Workshop	56
Tally Carter	58
Blue Bones	59
Tracing Loss	60
Blind Fish	61
Early Mourning	62
U.F.O.	63
Gold and Dust	64
Naglfar	65
Evening Ritual	66
Carrie's Dream	67
Emergency	68
Friday Crash	69
Escaping	71
Great Aunt Sally's Socks	72
My Son's Leaving	73
Rest Haven	74
Psyche's Indecision	75
July 4th Party	76
Clear View	77
Intermission Show	78
Ceremony	79
Oracle at Delphi: Two Possibilities	80
Crow Matinee	81
Hop's Hammer Toes	82
War	83
Aphrodisiac	84
Shadow Boxing	85
Circusville	86
Passing Time	87
Like a Slow Anthrax	88
Spring Fever	89

Auction	90
Lasting	91
Off Season	92
The Visit	93
Verbal Convolution	94
Jamestown Ferry Ride	95
Java and Jive	96
At the Same Time	97
Fall's Lure	99
Market Street Blues	100
On the Chesapeake Bay	101
Champions	102
For Men Only	103

Part 3: Power Play

Cast	106
Act I	107
Act II	115
Act III	121
Act IV	127
Act V	133

Glossary	137
About the Author	139

Preface

What is truly timeless is the unity of souls that can leap continents, send whispers across oceans, call on another to speak their secrets and tell their stories. The desire to be heard has power no human or space can contain.

Such it is with the group of African women, whose spirits found me by way of a travelling stranger who loaned me a book she had bought entitled *The Art of the Weya Women* by Ilse Noy. In the 1990s these women had been taught by Noy, a European artist, to weave narrative quilts and tapestries and to create paintings. This earned them money, freedom, and better lives. Known as the Weya project, it grew and continues today.

When I had to return the borrowed book, I had not completed my work; however, two years later an African student of mine in the United States sent to Africa and got me the same book. These were the only facts I had. As I read about their lives, studied their art, and stared into the eyes of these kindred spirits, stories emerged one by one. I wrote monologues using some African words, facts, and names taken from Noy's book; however, the stories are fictional.

Little did I realize how this work would be the piece I needed to understand my own life and mission. When I finished the Weya poems, they meshed with two other completed manuscripts I had worked on for years. I have come to realize we do not have to know the way; just keep going and doing. Eventually, we arrive. Everything in the universe is unfolding to perfection.

Part 1

Women of Weya

Manena

My name means *mountain*,
and everyone says that I am made of rock inside
because I never show how I feel.
No one has ever seen me cry.
Long ago I swore to be like a man.
I have a plan to change how women are treated like dogs.
No, worse; dogs are free. You see,

I have a daughter, who may be able to escape from here.
She will show the way and more will follow.
I have heard from women in Harare of places far away
where a woman is equal to a man.
She can even own land without being married.

My girl is very smart and strong.
I teach her to be brave and to dream
while I weave and hide money in a hole.
As soon as she is of age, I will send her over the mountains
with money to last until she finds her way.

My plan keeps my fingers moving faster than anyone else's.
I breathe no word to anyone but weave my story into a tapestry
I will send with her that only she will understand.

After she is gone, I will weave more secrets.
There will be twin women: one weeping, the other laughing.
I'll hide my child in every scene.
She is the small bird flying high.

Journey 1

When I was a born, no *nyamukuta* helped me into the world.
My mother had me by herself with only wolves for company.
She did not have the herbs to prepare a necklace for me
to wear around my neck for medicine. So she said I got a fever
and there was no *muti* in the wilderness either.
Wait. Let me go back before that.

Once my mother was a powerful and talented leader
of a weaving workshop until some people began to fall ill and die.
They accused her of witchcraft and ran her into the mountains.
She would not tell me how she became pregnant with me.
I don't think she knew— only that it was meant to be this way.

Our home was a large, dry *ninga*
where my mother taught me to survive.
My only playmates were rabbits and wolves, tigers, lions, goats.
When I was five years old, one day an old woman appeared.
I never knew her name so I called her Wise Woman.
She called me Destiny.

Every day for five years she taught me great powers before
she disappeared. I cried for weeks because I loved her.
The last time we were together she told me she had a vision
that I would travel very far both in this land and across oceans.
I would find an ancient secret of the Great Spirit.
It would be hard and lonely, but until I did, I would be restless.

So much depends on my success.

Ngozi

      (avenging spirit)

They say I am crazy.
I think, "Sometimes yes and no."
Fits come and go like wild wind.
All I know for sure is this:
I do not belong in this skin.
I remember the woman I used to be.

Before she worked in Weya in a dress shop,
happy to bring home money for her family.
Now when I sleep, a demon spirit takes over me,
a wicked scheme of some great enemy.
It seems like only a dream until I awake to pain.
It twists inside my head and drives me crazy.
I fall on my knees, and wrestle it until
my body is like snakes in fire. Demon speaks ugly words
from my lips. Mother and my sisters cry and pray for me.

I believe I am cursed because of my father's secret sin.
He is ashamed he does not make much money for us.
In a jealous fit, he killed the man that herded his cattle for years
when the man showed money he had won to my father.
No one knows I saw this happen from a distance.
Three days after the man was buried, the *ngozi* came over me—
maybe because I am my father's favored daughter
or maybe because I know and do not tell on him.
When I go to speak, I cannot.

My family took me to the *n'anga* and asked what to do.
He told them that one of us had done a great harm.
The *n'anga* said to put three black chickens and three black goats
into the deep forest and call the villagers to beat drums loud and long.
Whoever is guilty will be driven to confess.

I am afraid what will happen to my father.

Three Wives

Grandmother told us this old story
about a rich man who had two wives.

One day he went hunting but found nothing
but a big snake that he brought home dead.

He asked the second wife to cook it and she would not.
She said she was afraid of it.
Because she was beautiful, he let her be lazy.
So he asked the first wife, who agreed to make soup
if he would sleep with her that night and not the other wife.
She made and cooked it then left to get herself ready.

While she was out, the second wife put sticks into the pot.
At dinner time the second wife said she was sick and could not eat.
When the first wife served the meal, she was shocked when
her husband bit down on stick and broke a tooth.

The husband called the wives together and asked them,
"Did you put sticks in the soup?"
Both said no. He was so angry
he went to the *n'anga* to find out the truth.
The wise one told him what to do.

The husband took the two wives on a trip where they had to
cross a deep river. He told them to hold on to a rope but said
spirits declared that the one who had lied would fall in.

The second wife got almost to the end
before she fell in and drowned.
The man was very sad to lose his beautiful wife.

Chimurenga

>(War ending in 1980 when Rhodesia became independent
>of Zimbabwe)

I saw comrades beat a young woman on the back and bottom
and turned my head and put my hand over my mouth
so I would not scream. It was not because she was a prostitute
but that she fell in love with a policeman.

They also beat the *muroyi* and *vatengesi*.
Then they kill them if the *povo* agree it is so.
If a witch confesses her partners, they die, too.
Most tell lies because of they are jealous or angry
so whoever has more people on their side wins.

The comrades called us all to a *pungwe*,
and told us about the politics and the difference between them
and the soldiers. We made them food and gave them beer.
Then the comrades sent boys to get my best aunt.
She was not a witch but a good wife and mother of six children.
They killed her because someone said her son divorced his sister.

Then it got worse for us.
One night four *mujibhas*, acting like comrades,
came to our house and demanded money from my father.
They knew he was a teacher and asked for his pension.
When he said it had not come yet, they shot and killed him.
My mother started screaming, and this is all I remember.

Eveline

I did not know what is painting
and did not believe I will get
a lot of money as they said.
So I went to Magura to find out.
I passed a test. It was hard because
I had never drawn or used a brush.
After months of lessons, I was a real artist.

At first I just wanted money
but no more. I love my work.
Some women do not care so much,
but I take time to make each person different—
animals, too, but not so often.

I copy the style of Valente Malangatana.
He is famous Mozambican painter.
He made things look alive called three-dimensional.
Now the style has his name *Malangatana*.

I am careful to only paint nice things
in case someone sees their own face.
If I painted a bad truth about them,
I am afraid they would hurt me.
I want to be famous but not after death.

Journey 2

Just before she died, my mother made me promise
to go and look for the ancient lady I called Wise Woman.

When I left Mother's body in our *ninga*, I thought I would die, too.
Loneliness is worse than hunger.

I knew I had to leave the only home I had known for sixteen years.
It took me a while to say goodbye to my animal family.

They understood and mourned with looks.
I cried so much I thought I might not be able to stop.

I wandered down unsure until a lion came to me
and beckoned to follow him.

I thought the time it took to go down the mountain
must be what Mother meant by the word *forever*.

When we got to the bottom, it was dark night.
I laid down beside the lion and slept.

I dreamed my mother came to me in a shining light.
She said she would always be with me.

At daylight I awoke, and my lion guide was gone.
Where he had been, there was a smooth stone.

In my hand it was so warm, it felt like love.
I did not look back but walked on alone.

Kutando Botso

My oldest cousin was born with evil spirits inside just like his father.
His mother was afraid so she made excuses for her son
when he was young and got into trouble.
When he raped a neighbor's girl of only ten years,
his mother lied and said at that time
he was gone to Hare to buy goods.

One day my mother went to visit these relatives
and found her sister on the floor crying and holding herself
and with many bruises and cuts. She told that her eldest son
had done this while he was drunk—he thought she was a girlfriend.

When my father and uncles learned of it, they said the family sin
must stop with this son. They ordered him to work and pay money
for his wrong and to stay under their watch one year.
Not to be— this cousin was stubborn and ran away.
No one could find him.

After three months he became so sick he came back home
and agreed to do *kutando botso*. He had to go to homes singing,
kutando botso. Most villagers beat him, too.
Good, I say.

After the evil spirits were driven out of him, my father and uncles
brewed *hwahwa*. When the men all drank it, my cousin's bad deed
was erased. He was free to go home and live as a normal son.

I do not think any woman will marry him
unless an old and ugly one.

Sheela

I have a friend whose daughter Sheela
shamed her family. They say she was born wild.

For two years Sheela promised to marry a nice man
but changed her mind without good reason.
Then she got pregnant by a younger man.

The first man loved her still but was very angry.
He had given her many expensive things
like jewelry, furniture, store-bought clothes.
He came to demand pay-back for all.

Because Sheela had no money,
my friend and her husband had to pay
the old boyfriend with cattle worth $ 500.
This is the Shona law. Because of this trouble,

now their daughter must give them her firstborn child.
It is the Shona way.
Who knows if Sheela will obey?

Chenura

After a man is dead one year, ceremony begins
to decide who takes his wife.
His relatives gather *rapoko* to make strong beer
brewed by elder women without husbands.
Everyone drinks but only after offerings to spirits.

A cow is slaughtered and everyone eats according to rank.
They dance and drink all night before the wife (if allowed) decides.
So sad if she is not liked by the new husband's relatives
because they will chase her back home to her parents. Sometimes
they do this right then, and she must leave in the dark without
her belongings— especially if she has no young children.

If she has a big inheritance or is young and beautiful,
her dead husband's brothers will dress up to woo her.
No, it is not about love. Once in a while,

there will be a different woman strong like my mother.
She refused to take a new husband and gave up my father's
inheritance when family said she had to marry. At her *chenura*,

my mother declared her oldest son to act as our father.
Soon after when he married, she took care of us by herself.
She planted and harvested her own fields that grew
even when others withered.
Now everywhere she is respected for her good business head.

I will be like her, too, but I will not remain here.
I am sure there is much more to life somewhere out there.

Journey 3

I tucked the warm stone next to my heart to keep me strong
and walked a narrow road seeing new trees and bushes.

To help I hummed a small song Mother taught me about
how the sun and moon are the creator's eyes watching over us.

It seemed so long before I saw anything but bushes and land.
Finally in the distance something like big rocks but not.

I was afraid but curious and full of hope to see people.
I wondered if they would like me and help me.

Mother had explained that men look different especially.
Closer I saw what I thought she said were homes called huts.

I stopped and called hello, but no answer—nothing—
then a moving thing like a tiny tiger without stripes.

It watched me as I went from hut to hut.
All were empty— no food or anything.

I was sad until the little creature rubbed against my leg.
I knew I had a friend and named it *Upenyu*, which is life.

Suddenly in the distance I heard a noise like thunder but not.
"*Upenyu*," I said, "let us go to it."

Tima

I

I was a good wife and already mother of three
until I lost twin babies. They were most beautiful
I have ever seen. The boy came dead, but the girl was turned
wrong not to be born. When the *nyamukuta* finally pulled her out,
my baby opened once her big brown eyes, looked at me
as if to say, " I'm sorry," then went to sleep forever.
I passed out for two days and did not want to wake up.

I was afraid to lay with my husband. It is true,
I used the plant *nhanzva*— drank its roots in cold water
every time after he had his way with me. Still,
I got pregnant and always I am sick.

Elder women said it is rare for *nhanzva* not to work,
and I am being punished for sins. Also they said
I must let my man go to prostitutes and not complain.
I am a bad wife but don't know why.
I cry to think of him with other women.

II

So he goes too much, spends too much. In a few months
he gets sick and more sick. Then a doctor,
who came to our village, says he has AIDS.
I am filled with grief and guilt. I nurse him
and beg forgiveness. He would not speak to me until
on his deathbed. Then he tells me

I have been a good wife and nothing is my fault because
he has always been with prostitutes since first we married.
I want to die but cannot leave my children.
Even if this burden-baby is born alive,
it will not live long.

Unmarried

He spoke words of love to me in a foreign tongue
and made me dizzy like the first time I drank beer.
But the feeling was in my heart, not my head.

Maybe this is why I slept with the handsome Italian.
I was a domestic worker in his household,
and he promised he was going to marry me.
I did not use the precaution because I heard
if an unmarried woman does,
she will be cursed with no children.

When his contract came to an end, he left without me
right after I had his baby. At first he sent money
for the child but stopped after a year.
I thought about *kuzvisungirria* by drinking poison
but did not want to leave my son.

I had to go back to my parent's house to live
because I could not support us.
I go to Weya to learn appliqué so that
I can be both mother and father to him.

When he is older, I do not know how I will explain to him
why he looks so different— light skinned like his father.

Barika

Four years my husband and I are happy
until a second girl is born. He wants sons,
and I can tell now in his eyes he does not want me.

In Harare he found a young girl he asked to be second wife.
I hate her. She is pretty, and she cannot cook or clean.
He sleeps with her, not me. So I shun her completely
and tell my children to do the same.
This child-wife cried so much my husband beat me,
but I am strong and did not change.
Then he took us to the chief,
who said I must be good to her or else
the village elders will bring harsh judgment on me—
maybe send me away into the mountains.
I cannot win, and for my children's sake I obey.

Now she is pregnant, and my husband is excited for a son.
She is sick a lot, so he will return to my bed for his needs.
Tonight I will cook his favorite meal, deer meat,
and get him drunk to lay with me. I need to have a boy.
I dream of poisoning second wife, but it is wrong to kill a baby.
The spirits would seek revenge. She is so weak and lazy
that if a baby is born, it will be more work for me.
It would be best if she died. If not, at least I hope

she has a baby girl and then grows thin as a reed.
If so, maybe a big wind will blow her away.

Journey 4

We walked far until the sounds grew louder and louder.
I knew now it must be made by humans.

I think my heart joined the beat, *thumb- da- thumb, da- thumba- thumba.*
Then came what I'd longed for yet feared— voices.

I stopped, pulled out my stone, kissed it, and moved on.
Upenyu and I hid in the brushes where I stared amazed.

Maybe it was the smells of food or maybe destiny
made me step forward when all the sounds stopped.

When the people saw me, they stared— some backed away mumbling.
Maybe it was my skin-made clothes or just surprise.

One woman shrieked and fell backwards.
Later I found out she thought I was her dead daughter.

I spoke and they understood me enough
so that women gathered around to protect me.

They gave me food, clothes, and a bed of straw alone.
I think they believed I was not human but good.

Late that night in the dark I felt something warm beside me.
My only friend *Upenyu* had found me.

Silent One Speaks

Before when I had nothing, was nothing,
my husband caused fear inside me that burned like fire.
When he came home from drinking, I pretended
to be busy with chores until he fell asleep, if I was lucky.

He said he owned my body and mind if I had one.
Sometimes, he yelled at me, ripped my clothes off,
and knocked me to the floor. I will not say after that.

At first I cried and begged, but he laughed and did more.
I learned to stop all sounds, and soon he forgot I was.
I learned to forget myself, too. I thought I must be
too low to be human. I forget how long this went on.
Then he began to stay gone for days, weeks. One day

I wandered down the road and met women, who said they
were going to Weya. I had never left my village but I followed.
We learned to weave and make money. I made pictures
with stories I never spoke. I gave money to the husband
to send him drinking more and more. The rest I hid.
With every stitch I wove, I pretended to stab the needle
into the man I hated. Some might say

I made a kind of voodoo. Good. I don't care.
One day I realized the fire inside me was gone.
I started to laugh and couldn't stop for so long.
And guess what? The husband never returned. They say
now I talk so much it is hard to believe I was ever so dumb.

Ex-Combatant

They say the war is over.
Maybe for the country but not for women like me
who fought in secret. I was a leader in battles, so
I cannot go back home to be ruled by a husband.
Even if I must live alone, I will survive.

I was hero to all in my village then at only eighteen.
Now I do not belong because some women are jealous
or think I am wrong to be so bold.
Men are afraid because I am strong.
I think now I am more male than female.
Maybe I am neither one.

Still I could bear children, but after what I've seen,
why would I want to bring a child into this world?

Journey 5

They spoke so much like me I learned fast new things I'd never seen
like *ndiro* for eating off and a *mbikiza* made of cloth
they gave me to wear. It was a pretty red and soft.

They had been having a final *chipwa* to get rain—
drumming and dancing and chanting.
It did not come, so they would move to another place.

I told the women and the chief my family was dead.
Something told me not to say more.

They did not know what to make of me so treated me good.
Upenyu they thought was a *chikwambo*.

As we traveled for weeks, I noticed men looking much at me.
It was not a good feeling, so I stayed always with women.

Eventually, they found land near other villages to make their home.
I decided find out if new women could lead me to Wise Woman.

In a dream I saw my mother telling me to follow her.

Brother-in-Law

I was thirteen when a wealthy, old man
said he wanted me for a wife.
Because my father had seven girls, he agreed.
I begged and cried for days and nights, but it did no good.

The husband smells like a dead dog left to rot in the sun.
I would rather eat cow dung and *zongororo* than kiss him.
I still close my eyes when he comes near me.
He gets his way, and I get nothing.
Already I have two girls.

He has a young brother who is single and good looking.
He visits and stays with us a lot.
At first he was just family, but he became a friend
because he felt sorry for me.

After time when the husband went out of sight,
his brother held me and kissed me.
I kept my eyes wide open.
At first I felt wrong, but we fell in love.

Now he begs me to run away with him and take the children.
I know it is wrong and very dangerous,
but is it not also wrong to live a life of misery?

Longing for him nests in my mind and gnaws like hunger.
I could wait for the old husband to die, but I am afraid
his brother will not.

Karua's Dilemma

I don't want to be a woman
who dies without having a child.
There would be no *chenura*
so my spirit will wonder alone forever.
The living will tie a rat on my back
or a sausage from a mumvee tree or a maize cob.
My whole life would be for nothing.

So my husband and I are taking all
of our money to get healing from a *n'anga*.
If it works, I hope for five children.
If not, there is no need for me to live much longer.
I might as well poison myself
because his family will find a way to kill me.
Already I see it in their eyes.

Motosai

While I brew beer with my mother,
I think about things like religion, other worlds,
and stories I want to write.
I don't talk about this because my family believes I am
wrong to question anything or wonder.
Once or twice I told Mother my thoughts and she said,
"Stay busy and you won't think so much.
All you need to learn is how to be a good wife and mother.
Get a rich husband so you won't have to work hard like I do."

So why did the creator give me this brain?
I don't need it to do women's work.
Even my poor, dumb cousin Never can do this.
I hate it and in the fields worse.
I don't want to marry, but my family
would call me crazy not to have children.

I want to be an artist in Weya
and be free to learn everything.

Maybe later I will adopt a child.

Journey 6

At first it was much to see and learn that I never imagined.
After a while, time dragged on like a useless shadow.

I learned about lives of people young and old, good and bad
but nothing about how to find Wise Woman.

I will go to the place I heard so much about from women.
No need to tell anyone; better to keep them wondering about me.

I know I can find Weya.
Upenyu will help me.

Annie

I was a prostitute in the cities, and I am not
ashamed because it was all I could do.
I had only a little education.
My mother before me and her mother were.

My customers were rich businessmen,
who treated me very nice—maybe because
I was pretty and had a good body.
I only took a few men and kept the same ones to be safe.

One not married fell in love with me.
He got so jealous I had to make him go away.

Once the wife of my best paying customer sent a spy
to catch us having sex. The husband paid him a lot
not to tell, but I got worried and let this one go, too.

I got tired of problems and decided to move to Hare.
I had enough money for a while so I looked for a different job.
I met a man who hired me just to sit and welcome people
at the entrance of his office building. I think he liked my looks.
It was a good idea because we married soon.

I never want him or my children to know about my sex work.
I have a good life, and I want my daughters to be well educated.
I think it is the only safe way for women.

Most of the time I stay at home
because I fear I may meet someone I used to know.

Efo

Two years ago my young, pretty sister got sick fast
so bad she turned gray and was skinny as a reed.
Doctors in the hospital could not find the problem.
When they said she would die, we sent for Efo to come.

As soon as he saw her, he said, "Voodoo!"
He put his mouth on her head for a few minutes,
and she opened her eyes. This is all he did.
Efo told her," Get up and walk." She did.
We laughed and cried and gave Efo money.

Doctors begged him to go from room to room
and heal this one and that one very sick.
Efo always first prays to God.
No one else we know has so much power.
He can even work miracles from far away.
No minister I know can do that.

Don't ask me what Efo is.
Nobody knows.

Journey 7

I will not dwell on the long journey to Weya
except to say I found I had more friends than one.

How they knew I'm not sure. I think animals
speak a language that travels fast in the air
from one to another to another— even in some cases
for humans like me.

I found them everywhere to guide me.
When I arrived at the training center, the stone next to my breast
grew warmer. They made a place for me to stay.
Day after day, as women told me their stories,
I listened and sought the wisdom in each one.
Their lives and dreams poured onto their art,
took life in the telling.
Is this all I am to learn? "No," came the answer from somewhere.
So I asked if anyone knew a special wise woman.
Yes, but it was their art teacher, not the one I sought.

I went to a quiet place to be alone and sit with one question,
What next?

Filis

Everyone thinks I am a bad daughter
because I ran away from my husband.
If they knew why, they would not say so;
but if I tell, I could die.

His parents demanded the *lobola* paid back,
but my father did not have enough.
So his family burned all my parents' chickens and firewood.
I told my father I am going to Weya and learn a craft to repay them.
I will do appliqué because men are not so good at this.

I can make a picture to show my husband was not a real man
because he wanted other men and not me.
I saw the way he looked at them and more.

Once I came home early from visiting my sisters in Harare
and caught him naked with a young boy.
The boy grabbed his clothes and ran. My husband
beat me and said he would kill me and my family if I told.

Ella

I am in trouble for falling in love
and marrying with a man not Shona.
My family is angry so they demand him $2,000 for my *lobola*
They know my husband cannot pay, so they still rule me.

It gets worse as the days go on. Now doctors say I must be cut open
for our first child to be born, but my parents they say no.
They think it is my punishment, and I cannot go against the spirits.

If my baby and I die, my parents will not let us be buried
unless the *lobola* is paid. This is my great fear because
our spirits will never rest. My father says something bad
will happen also to my husband to avenge the baby's spirit.

I try to think good and pray for mercy. If we live,
the three of us will run away to Hare. Yes, it is wrong
but my parents will not take my first born.
In Hare I can go to the Weya Training Center
and learn to make money. I will give it
to my husband to pay *lobola* for me.

I don't care if I never see other family again.
I will make my own and be good to them.

Journey 8

Now that I have met many people,
the only way I know how I am different
is that I am always protected
and humans and animals give me whatever I need.
This is not so for the others I see everywhere.
They are driven by fears and wants, it seems.
Some have no purpose as I do.

I walk past a shop and stop as the stone warms on my skin.
I go inside. Shelves are packed with crafts like carvings
of lions, elephants, zebras; drums, knives, bowls;
colorful bead necklaces and bracelets and pins.

I spy hanging on a back wall alone a small quilted square.
In it a woman reaches for a star and mountains in the distance.
My heart beats fast as the stone almost burns.
I know who made each stitch with pride and love.

The shopkeeper sees my gaze and takes it down,
but to my surprise walks away from me.
I ask if it is for sale and she says, "No. Just sold today.
I will pack it to mail."

"Can you tell me who and where it goes?"

"Yes. A business in the United States."

I ask to see who and where and she agrees.
I feel the energy drain from me as I walk away.
I know this is the clue I need, but is it taken from me.

Mr. Mudzingwa's Death

Even before the drumming woke me at midnight,
I knew that my father-in-law would be dying.
I saw it in a dream two days ago but kept it to myself.

I even went to the fields to gather *musosawafa*
leaves for everyone to wash their hands and faces
after the funeral. You see,

I have strange powers I must hide because a woman
cannot know things like the *n'anga*. Elders would say
I am a witch and drive me into the mountains to die.

Yet I know that Mr. Mudsinga was killed by a spirit
to avenge his daughter who drowned herself last month.
No man would marry her because she acted dumb.

What they don't know is that her father had his way
with her since she was a little girl. This I saw in the dream
that made me rise in the night and go outside.

Now I must hide my happiness so that my husband
does not see. I will cry loudest at the funeral
but it will be for his poor sister.

Brema

My father patched huts, and my mother and I
raised and sold chickens and tomatoes. Little brother
was too young to work, and we were poor.
When my father died, I decided to quit school
and went to learn painting in Mukute
because the Mukuteans are not jealous like in Weya.

I lived with two other young girls and sent money
home to my mother and young brother.
But in my village they are jealous of us.
They tell that my friends and I are eating meat and sleeping
with many husbands, but it is not so— at least not with us.

One day my uncle came to Mukute and said my mother
is very sick. I go home and find she is dead,
but no one tells me what was wrong. Then my brother
wakes me in the night and says he believes our uncle
killed her to make me come home. It is custom
he would take us into his household.

We fear him, so my brother and I ran away in the night.
I went to a witchdoctor and got voodoo.
He mixed a powder of leaves and ashes
and more things I don't know what.
I paid him for the strongest to keep the uncle away.

Now my brother and I live in Mukute with my friends,
and I send him to school. I got $200 for my last painting.
Then I made a picture of my uncle killing my mother,
and gave it to the witchdoctor to keep. He is so happy for it
I think he may put a death curse on my uncle.

Journey 9

Wise Woman said I would cross the seas
so I find a cruise ship going to USA.
I have no money to pay so I ask the women
I know for help. They will give me money
now for the fare. I will find the buyer whose
name and number I memorized in the shop.
Then she will buy directly from them.

What about *Upenya?* They will keep him
until I return, which I explain to him.
He would not like the long ride over water,
but I will feel so alone.

As soon as I step aboard, the stone warms.

Uroyi

      (Witchcraft)

We Shona are jealous people.
This is the only way to protect yourself.
Women cannot be strong or too good at anything,
so the way to get what you want is *uroyi*.

I suspect my husband has a girlfriend in the city,
so I go to see, and it is so. I am not a *muroyi*,
but I am sure to make friends with one that lives nearby.

I prepare strong *hwahwa* and a fat *hanga* and take
them to the *muroyi*. I ask her to cast a spell—
make his girlfriend have *kuoma rupandi*.
I know my husband will leave her and come home.

Then I will give him *mupfuhwira* to make him
carry the maize and grind the *rapoko* and make love.
He will obey me even when I hit him.

Gudza

This is a picture of my brother,
but he should not have been born.
His mother called herself my mother's best friend,
but this woman was sleeping with my father.
When I heard she was pregnant by him,
I went to her house and beat her.
There was a lot of blood on her face.
I did this for my mother; she is not a fighter.

I screamed at my father, too, and asked him,
"How can you do this?" I kept on until
he sent me to live with an aunt that summer.
Later I came home and fell at his knees crying,
and we forgave each other.

My sisters and I love our brother.
He is a very good person.

Kufamaba Famba

     (Prostitution)

They call me *Beauty* because I am so ugly
no one would marry me. I have gap teeth
and a hard, square face. I look like a man.

I went to a *n'anga* who said I am punished
because my mother slept with men of the village
when my father took a job in the city.

The *n'anga* gave me medicine and said go to a *mumvee* tree
and sing a song. Soon I had very big breasts men like.
I got long legs they like also.

I could live and work in a Christian church,
but I like men and sex better. My partners
treat me good because I am not the wife.

I live in a hut left by a family that said
it was haunted by evil spirits, but I do not fear.
I make them offerings I know they like.

Once I awoke in the night when the moon was bright.
I went outside saw a black rhinoceros. I offered him
maize and asked for a sign of my future.

In the morning I went to see what he left me.
In the dirt he had pawed me a message.
I read it and jumped up and down laughing.

Journey 10

Deep sleep filled me as soon as the ship set sail,
so the long trip passed like a dream.
Maybe it was God's comfort mixed with exhaustion
I had denied; maybe also boredom from confinement.
I did not resist the great water like a mother's comfort.

When I stepped onto the place called America,
 I was not afraid—only amazed at everything,
especially so many white skins and others I had never seen.

I'm sure I looked lost for a woman approached me
and to my surprise said, "Hello. My name is Madeleine.
Do you need any help?"
When I told her where I came from and why,
she smiled, "Yes. I know about the Weya artists.
Come home with me. You will see."
It was then the stone at my breast almost burned.
I followed her gladly to her home.
It was dark before we arrived, and she led me to a small room
and told me to rest. Once again I slept in peace.

When morning light awakened me, the first thing I saw
hanging on the wall in front of me
was the same quilt square I had tried to buy in Weya.
I called to my hostess, "Please tell me.
What do you know about this picture?"

Madeline said, "I was told that it is old, and the artist probably dead.
I found it on the internet and it comes from Weya."

Then I knew Mother is watching over me.

Runyoka

There is a secret forest below a mountain
where voices can be heard.
Some say trees talk; some say spirits.
It is only innocent people who died
given voices to plan revenge. I know.

I have heard my father and mother speaking.
They were murdered one night in our home
by freedom fighters during the *Chimurenga*.

Three men locked my brother and me in a room.
They said my father was a sellout, but it was not true.
While they beat him to death, my mother begged, cried
and screamed for us to run away.

My brother and I climbed out of the window
and ran and ran until we came to this secret forest.
We cried ourselves to sleep. At dawn, we heard

first Mother whisper they were in good place
always watching over us. She told us go to her sister.
Then Father told us his brother's sons made
the lie to get his money, and we should not go back.
He said revenge would come;
then we could go home and claim everything.

Katesi

My painting is the story of a dream.

As a child I had bad headaches
that made me blind, but visions came.
Children made fun of me, so I had friends in my head—
wild jackals, lions, and kudus, who loved me.

My parents took me to the *n'anja*.
He told them it was voodoo from an enemy
of my father or mother. Not so.
The *n'anga* gave me bitter medicine
that put me in a trance so he could call the demon out.
I slept so long they thought I was dead.
It did not work, but that night I had a bad dream.

Mangwana-Mangwa, great lion of Chazezesa, came to me.
He said warn the men in our village
to stop killing the kudu and jackals in his area.
He was so angry I was frightened.
When I woke up, I told my family the dream.
They did not believe even though I cried and begged.
My eyes got worse, even at home.

One day at school my head felt like an explosion,
and I passed out. When I woke up, I was home.
I heard the drums and saw the men coming
from the forests carrying someone covered in blood.
I knew before my mother started wailing,
that my brother Chipezvero was dead and why.

Journey 11

For the next few days I told Madeline everything
from life on the mountain to my quest for Wise Woman
and the secret she bid me find. All the while she
listened as though she had waited a lifetime to hear it.

When I finished, I said, "Now tell me your story, Madeleine.
I know I am meant to hear."

She nodded and replied, "Of course. Before you came,
I did not understand my life; even now it is clearer.
So it will be for you and others to discover
that the answer lies in living the question.

"Be patient; my story will take a long time—it has two parts.
Nothing in a life can be omitted to understand it.
But I promise you that by the time
we get to the end, you will have the answer you seek."

Part 2

Java and Jive

Supplication

The door is opening.

As you wait for the face,
imagine a slender woman
dressed in black tulle,
red lips smiling.

You'll meet one night
when the moon is full,
the air so still that the only sound
is the ticking of a clock.

Do not be alarmed
when her white arms unfold,
the gilded fingernails beckon.
She is the answer to your prayers.

Tell her everything.
She won't tell or disappear
but untangle years of wiry lies
that strangle your dreams.

As you speak, be sure to stare into her eyes
where you'll see yourself transform
into someone you should know.

Trying Not To Be Born

I was born upside down
out of natural reach.
Mama labored fourteen hours
in hot pain.
I fought hard
clinging to her swollen flesh.
When she stopped breathing,
I gave in. My fingers slipped
in fright, lost their grip.
Mama gasped and I began
the fall to death.
I screamed.
Then the cut,
the final separation.

In this world I struggle
upside down.
I must be careful always
to hide a tiny scar
on my heel.

Confessing My Father

Did you say, "Good night," when you meant,
"Goodbye," the night you died upstairs?
They left me at Aunt Edna's to play
while everybody buried you except me.
I only saw them lower you in nightmares.

Sometimes I see you on your hands and knees crawling,
peeping around corners, grinning, me squealing.
Why are you hiding? What are you holding back?

Mama pulls out the wooden cigar box of family pictures, sighs,
"I remember your Daddy in the old store on Main Street.
Working fourteen hours a day, smoking, and taking BC's
is what killed him so young."

I only remember you in a long, white apron on Sunday mornings
cracking eggs in a black frying pan.
I'm sitting at the enamel top table watching steam rise .
I wonder why I crack men like those shells?

Daddy, why can't I remember any words you said to me?
Not even the only picture of you I'm in
tells me anything I need to know.
Sitting on the living room sofa,
your arms scare-crowed over our shoulders,
my sister and you are smiling,
so why have I been crying?

If I go to your grave and fall down
on my hands and knees and dig six feet
into my heart, will I find you?
If I do, will you let me in?

Trauma

My third summer paralyzed behind the checkout counter
in uncle's grocery store. I'm standing at the register
frozen like the Brown Mule bars in the ice cream chest.

Uncle roams aisles from canned goods to dried beans, rice
mumbling, chuckling. I'm wondering where Joe, the meat cutter is.
He always gave me cheese when this was Daddy's store before he died.
I'm too shy to ask or say anything.

I don't know why suddenly I feel warm pee running down my legs
onto the dingy tile floor. Everything stops here.
I feel cold, numb, and it seems a long way to the bathroom.
What happens after that I wonder?

Did I stay or run home through the back fields?
Did ever go back to the store?
It's like walking out in the middle
of a bad movie you try to forget.

Since then, so much has hardened in my mind,
still thawing slightly when particles of love shine on its dark tundra.

Gray Barn

    for L.D. and Butch

The brown speckled hens flopped
slinging puddles of blood in the dry dirt.
When we had thrown away the dumb-eyed heads,
my cousins and I tried to smoke pieces
of hay behind the gray barn. We fussed
about how Grandma was going to make us wash
ourselves again, pick feathers to stuff pillows,
go to bed at dark; but we wouldn't go to sleep.

One night I dreamed we had gone to heaven,
where we ran down the road towards Iola's house.
She sat on a porch of gold, smiling at us and waving.
We played there all day, and Iola fed us fried apple pies.
Grandma watched from behind the gray barn
stuffing clouds with feathers.

The Devil's Workshop

    after Maxine Kumin's *The Nightmare Factory*

this is the hell you've heard of
the devil's forge
the blacksmith of tortures
he swivels you on a spit
he skins you with a razor inch by inch
he rips your veins with needles
his black claw
is coiled with an asp
like Cleopatra's bracelet

these are Satan's tools
that breed from the fire
his foul breath feeds the
flames crawl your raw flesh
your bones glow in the dark
his chamber knife bevels your skull

these are his angels
they evoke screams
in any language
Jack the Ripper sculpts
London sluts
Hitler bakes Jews for supper
Lucrecia serves poison wine
Manson's women wash in blood
rapists ride erect
on high society ladies

hour after hour
evangelists rivet the news
to pockets of the faithful
your white hot heart erupts
a new cancer festers in every cell
it oozes through your pores
Satan jacks open your mouth
and pours shit down your throat

here in this black hole
he slices fat from your belly
and sprinkles it with salt
through cracked lips you cry

Lazarus, for Christ sake a drop of water
Lazarus, go tell my brothers and sisters
who live with hookers and dealers
waiting to brand them
with Satan's sign
like stamping endless
deposit slips.

Tally Carter

How have you spent your life, ancient lady?

"I've been searching old, empty wells."

What was your quest?

"To find a boy named Tally Carter
I lost in a childhood dream."

What have you found?

"This glass box scarred with wishes
contains his book of lies.
It begins on the page that is missing.
The story has faded with age
except for a cottage of ashes
scattered on the last page."

Where will you go from here?

"Over that mountain I hear Tally calling.
When you find him what will you do?

I'll go down singing a lullaby
and bear him a cross of bones."

Blue Bones

She stands on the deep edge of her pool
drinking another martini

> *Once there was a fish*
> *who swam to Kingdom Come,*
> *and by the end of the day*
> *became blood in the blue*

watching shadows ribbon under water. One emerges.
Drowned in his violet eyes, she sips, swallows, presses the tip
of her tongue into the olive's fleshy center. He swoops her up,
glides through glass doors into her bedroom

where he lays her down and disappears. Alone again
she stares at clothes crammed in her closet:
restless blouses, pants, jackets rearrange themselves by colors.
Static electricity, sparks fly, jazzing the room.

Her red satin dress swirls through the air and cascades onto her body.
She is in a nightclub dancing with every man until dawn.

She sits at her desk, sips strong coffee,
gazes at the void on the blue screen, and types

> *Gentlemen:*
>
> > *In regard to the balm of Gilead*
> > *that I ordered...*

She slumps deeper into blue
silk sheets and
dreams of a fish
who scrapes his belly
on the bottom
of the sky.

Tracing Loss

It takes coming back to the scene thirty years later:
the bridge across the Rivanna River,
the lone, twisted road that leads to an old stone jail,
and past our family graveyard. A few
miles more, and I'll cross a smaller bridge
that runs over the tiny town of Bremo Bluff,
where I've sat in the funeral parlor more than once.

I pull in at the country store where Daddy always stopped
Sundays to buy us ice cream cones as we wound
home from his parents' farm deep in Fluvanna County.
Even then his face was intent on getting back
to endless work that drove him to early death.

An old magnifying glass paperweight on my desk
advertises *Atlantic Casket and Coffin Company*.
I place it on my left palm and see the Rivanna
cut my lifeline in two.

Blind Fish

Out of contempt for a dry life
I became a mermaid.
I speak the bubbled language of fish.
Coding and decoding,
I am their only interpreter.
Bound by tight fins,
I am numb from the waist down.
In my hand I hold a silver dagger
the only defense my father left me
before he disappeared.

One day I hit bottom, my heart brined, thirsty.
I follow the ghostly green light of an Angler fish
into the lair of the dreaded Loligo.
Something kin stirs my blood.
My father, a Benthos, crouches in a corner,
victim of his own blindness.
With monstrous tentacles
the Loligo gropes for him,
its horny beak poised to rip and gulp.
I grab my dagger and stab.

Still without vision
Father allows me closer
than before his death.
But when I reach to touch him,
He shivers back.

I slit the veil between us.

Father, don't be afraid.
Let me touch the empty sockets.
You will no longer be blind,
and I will become human again.

Early Mourning

A woman died today too early
before she could reach for the morning
paper lying at her doorstep
before she could sip Maxwell House coffee
hot on the stove
before she could make the daily call
to her daughter Marie.

Death slipped in the back way
and found her still in her nightgown.
She lies on a white crocheted spread
waiting for the mortician, who slept
late this morning.

Marie fumbles through a closet
for her mother's favorite dress
savors her White Shoulders cologne
while neighbors drink coffee
small-talk around her Formica top table.

Outside, garbage men clank tin cans
their brisk voices echoing in chilly
morning air.

U.F.O.

Driving home, I spy it first gliding on a midnight sky—
big egg-shaped craft with tiny braided lights cascading down it.

"What in the world? A flying Christmas tree?"
I exclaim to my sleeping son beside me.

He lifts his head, mumbles, "Piece of moon, I guess."

"No! Wrong shape. Sit up and look."

"Whoa! Hey! Wait a minute! Pull over, Mom."

I slow down, swerve into a county store lot and we watch
until the whatever-it-is coasts out of sight.

Next day I call General Wilson, retired secret agent to Russia,
who declares, "I believe you. I'm going to Washington tomorrow.
I'll report it to the Air Force Defense Department.
Be prepared for a lot of questions."

Two weeks later I get a form letter.

The rest is history and news on the front page of our town paper.
Wherever I go, someone asks, "Aren't you the teacher who saw the UFO?"
My son and I grow tired of being celebrities, and the feds never call.

Now I 'm glad I never told anyone about the two silent passengers
riding that night in the back seat of my car.

Gold and Dust

I find it nested in a small porcelain box shaped like a casket
with tiny yellow and pink flowers painted on top—
a gold locket bracelet, gift to Mother from my father.
Beside it her high school ring
with a woman's ivory head in a cracked, onyx set.

I stretch the tarnished accordion band over my hand,
then open the heart hoping to find a secret— a folded note, a picture.
I stare at its emptiness, aware of the cold metal squeeze.
I want to feel the pinch, understand why Mother held
no more treasures next to her skin.

After his death, she married a man numbed by war
and unknown to her before they wed, impotent.
For years she suffered like one confined to an open tomb.
When she broke her arm, she carried it around
wrapped, pinned and cradled like a baby.

Without the oil of love she'll never mend—
her skin dry and thin, bones brittle.
I imagine her falling again and again,
a pattern of fracturing that crazes her nerves, her mind.
I fear in time she will not die but crumble.

Naglfar

It's a ship of fingernails,
the shopkeeper muses,
smiling at the painting.
An old Norse Legend says
it carries lost souls to a land of torment.
The cloud-ringed island of the past
is alive with fire. You think

of the faces on the ship
as you browse the room. You stare
into a beveled-edged mirror,
see the little sister who loved her looks.
You bargain the price,
step out into the street,
carrying your secret under your arm.
As you pass an ancient woman in furs,
you stare at her glossy nails.
Will she sail from the smoke-filled city
without warning?

In your basement you place the picture
face down on the highest shelf.
You know it never existed.

Evening Ritual

Lean closer to the mirror, mask my skin with ivory,
paint wide red strokes around anxious lips.

Clown-face cheeks, draw eyes around eyes, shadow lids with silver.
Slip into a black dress and ankle-strapped high heels.

Tip toe into the mirror and shed my self.
Slither out the back door, into the night.

Hurry toward distant streetlights,
giant matches that ignite longing.

Hush heartbeat! Listen!
Poignant songs of promises.

The clock strikes midnight, echoing silence.
Run fast-backwards, back to the door, mirror.

Sit at the dresser, cream away my spirit,
Stare at the naked face, turn away.

Shrink into my other. Outside
my shadow waits, shivering in moonlight.

Carrie's Dream

Song breezes strum black
strands of Carrie's hair as
she saunters down the road
dust powdering bare feet.
Keys jingle on twine
that binds her waist.
She roams with the full moon
seeking to unlock the right door
to step inside another woman's body.
She already knows how
to be a lady as seen on TV.
She would lie
in a blue, round tub
soak away all traces of dirt
emerge smelling of lilacs, hair shining.
Then pull the plug
rinse old skin down the drain,
slip into a satin robe.
Like Cinderella her clean feet
would slide into fancy slippers.
As for the man, he would be glad she came
noticing only the change
in his wife was good
like fresh, soft bread.

Emergency

The tornado spins towards our house,
and I am not dressed to die.
Mother said always be prepared.
Musky smell of death swells in stagnant air.

I run to my son's room calling his name.
He has become the wrestler Ric Flair.
Black sunglasses slide off his face— he has no eyes.
"Don't worry," he laughs. "In this disguise I can beat anything."

Our deaf neighbor, a witch, bursts through the door,
snatches his ears, hisses, "I have the daughter you never conceived."
She knocks me to the floor. We grapple until she rolls over
and becomes my dead father. Grinning, his face cracks,
turns into a lead crystal vase I broke and hid.

I scream.

My husband, locked inside the bedroom, wakes from a dream,
breaks down the door, and pushes me to the basement stairs
where I fall headfirst and land beside a coffin.

Inside it a heart beats, and someone whispers my name.

I lift the lid.

Friday Crash

for Grace Simpson

I yank off my face,
hang it on the doorknob,
turn the lock and stop the clock.

End of a wicked week
that feels like a hangover I don't deserve,
caught like a summer cold.

I find myself leaning, almost falling
off the chair. I try to sit up straight,
but my head is heavy, my brain sliding.

I look back at the face
for any sign of change.
It sags, pleated like a hand fan,
mouth agape, ready to scream.

Maybe this weekend
I'll go into hibernation,
finish *Finnegan's Wake*,
eat a dark chocolate cake.

I brew ginseng tea,
gift from Ming
for teaching him English.
"It has powers," he said.

I find two cups from the Chinese restaurant
where one summer Grace and I
sipped magic potions
stirring out poems from the leaves.

Continued...

I fill my cup and hers, too,
step out of my body and toss it
down the laundry shoot.

I drink a toast to Grace, to Ming,
to black cats and orange dahlias.

Escaping

Reading this poem will cost you your life.
I steal from you time I have lost.
How many heartbeats?

Son of Dionysus, you drugged me with wine-soaked lines
until I became a Maenad at your command. One day
you laughed at my dancing, and I ran into forbidden woods,
followed twisted vines of tangled dreams into my future
where I saw everything.

I was old lying on a speed bump in a parking lot.
You left your apartment, rode down the elevator
and climbed into a black coupe. Slowly, you ran over me
until I was dead. As you drove away, I revived young.

Fireflies in my brain, blinking visions of you
robed in snakeskin sitting erect on a throne of steel.
A crown of eyes orbits your head. I stand before
a smoke-shrouded window knowing I will shatter
the panes and destroy your image.

Great Aunt Sally's Socks

She tugs one sock
watching her hammer toe
stare through a hole
crooked like a squash;
no more a part of her
than the yellow sock
sagging on her bony leg
like the chicken necks
she longs to twist again.
She'd feed them crumbs by rows
and before she could finish one
they were ready to eat again:
like pulling up this baggy sock
the yellow color of gravy
her daddy used to sop with biscuits.
He would eat a hen at one meal
then suck marrow from its bones.
Once she could suck her big toe
now covered with knots.
She had tried to tie the knot once
but got cold feet same as now.
Her daddy's feet were white as dough.
He always blessed their daily bread
and wore white socks when he died.
Now she wonders as she sits on the edge
of this cold, metal bed:
is she the virgin mother of her father
is she dead?

My Son's Leaving

What's left after motherhood that taught me all
I ever knew of love? Soul insists there's more—
that I must slip out the door right behind you,
leave and never look back. If I do, I'll turn to stone.
Already I'm tomb cold, numb to my bones.

Years ago without a home, we two deserted children
clung to one another. Medicated, I moved as a sleepwalker,
while you, poor baby, cried day and night absorbing my fears.
All I could do was rock you, rock myself
to appease the anguished mute razing our nerves.

A second marriage and seventeen years we existed in a museum—
rooms of stolid antiques with a petrified man,
a statue carved from losses. On pills again,
I almost killed myself trying to make us a home.

Now alone anesthetic memories swell inside me:
you this, you that, you everywhere.
Curly haired toddler ask to wash dishes,
stand on a stool tossing foam, mumbling, "Not fun."
Nights at your bedside I tuck you under warm covers,
create stories about Funky Monkey you cuddle
until you fall asleep, then kiss your cheek and linger.

When you left for college, I felt my life bleeding
drop by drop by drop.
My only child, my only reason to smile— gone?
My head says, "Let go," but heart cleaves
like a weeping willow's last leaf.

Rest Haven

Annie stares through a window trying to remember:
criss-cross crusts on cherry pies
red checkered tablecloths at church suppers
tomatoes ripening in the kitchen window
sunsets from their wicker rockers.

Where are those old December days:
ginger-scented mornings and cedar evenings
by the fire with snow falling, embers glowing
and Christmas coming?

Outside this no place she wants to be,
old children sit in rows squabbling over bingo.
Nurse calls out numbers but no one wins.

Sudden storm—dark shadows shroud the lawn.
Annie pulls a sheet over her head. Sleep.

She is gliding through the open window
and bright sky, rising higher.
Nurse runs after her calling,
"Annie, Annie, can you hear me?"

Far away Annie nestles in a warm, plump cloud.
Smiling, she tosses her famous ginger cookies
to hands reaching up from everywhere.

Psyche's Indecision

Of course I think my wonderful lover
cannot be a monster with human voice
disguised by a clever, selfish mother
to favor gods who gamble on my choice.
When my sisters visit, their doubts hook
my ego, feed my fears until I waver
desiring one unknown forbidden look.
Can love exist without truth? He'll never
suspect I lit this candle while he slept—
one glimpse to flee or stay forever. Why
remain a victim, lose my self- respect,
risk imprisoning future women's lives?
There's nothing but fear stands in my way.
I must not waver but my will obey.

July 4th Party

On a friend's deck overlooking the James River,
I watch poplar, oak, and hickory branches scrawl
geometry lessons on a blazing sky. Below
tree of heaven cloaks the sloping ground.

It's already 105 in the shade. Heat makes
my mind hazy, body lazy as I mingle
with husbands, wives, cousins. I feel
the sweat of being single. Not even
the matriarch's chocolate earthquake cake
appeases my isolation.

Late afternoon humidity stagnates the air.
Elm leaves droop like parched tongues
begging for shallow, brown water.
The river seethes with dark shadows,
and cicadas' voices sizzle. Heavy haze
sheathes the mountain peaks.
Everything's sedated.

After slow goodbyes, I drive winding
country roads to the main highway home.
Alone, I lie uncovered, cannot sleep—
afraid my dreams of love might smother.

Clear View

I gaze at the back of a metal chair until it's a blur;
the cup and saucer carved in the center, the words
Mill Mt. Coffee and Tea merge, whirl. Nothing else
wants to stir inside or out, least of all me.

I'm wondering how I'll get myself to the gym today.
The weight of a heavy summer love has sprained my heart.
I need to pump up my brain, ready my muscles to maintain
enough energy to keep me from falling into a deep valley sleep.

A woman's hands contort in the air
motioning the waiter approaching me.
He plops down a white plate with a round scoop of chicken salad
ringed with purple onion, stacked high atop lettuce,
carrots and ruby tomatoes.
It sits staring at me, waiting for a blessing.

I turn away to the windows, see mountain peaks
fading in heavy August haze
behind masses of green trees clustered like full broccoli heads.
Three mustard-yellow stoplights swing slowly—
mute chimes in a thick, mocking breeze.

I reach for my glass of iceless water, hold it up to the light.
The lemon slice is a limp smile floating upside-down.
I poke it with my straw; it rolls over and grins.
A few fleshy pieces drift towards the bottom, sure to settle
before another old yellow sun slips behind Hunting Hills.

It reminds me to let go of my sultriness,
to write out what remains negative of men in my life,
Kamikazes hovering over their graves.
I watch their sunset descent,
my lips smiling open.

Intermission Show

>   at *The Nutcracker Suite*, Richmond, VA

Act 1: Inside the Ladies Lounge

Among ladies decked in holiday dresses, a homeless woman enters
silent as dust, and our chatter hushes as we pretend not to see her
shuffle to a corner and place a worn duffle bag on the floor.
Back pressed against a wall, she begins a seductive solo—
unbuttoning a faded blouse, sliding off baggy slacks.
As though we are blind or invisible,
she poses in dingy underpants and bra
before she pulls wrinkled clothes from her bag.

One by one we slip out of the door
and leave her preparing to go on alone.

Act 2: The Long Ride Home

In dark silence and full of nameless hunger,
I wonder at the street woman's silent show:
how her cumbersome moves made the sugar plum fairies' routines
airy cotton candy beside dark chocolate truffles.

Ceremony

Another dreary year dissolves.
I build a pyre on my soul's shore,
kneel to burn what remains
of another love lost this lifetime.

From underneath my breasts
I release that old bleeding heart image,
give it a goodbye kiss, and cast it into the fire.
Crackle, spit. It hisses resistance.

I do not breathe as it burns
but wait like one witnessing an execution.
Finally, black smoke chokes its last breath.
"Ashes to ashes, dust to dust."

I stand up amazed as I watch
a red dove rising from the blaze.
She folds her wings, slides inside of me
the way an arm slips into a silk sleeve.

Oracle at Delphi: Two Possibilities

I.
Perched like a wingless bird on a hard tripod, the beloved Apollo's pet, you could not have escaped what you felt so long ago: that sudden chill in the air, a tongue in your ear. Silk lips kissing yours as water from Lethe rippled down your throat. When they nibbled over you like a hungry fish, you moaned. Then the thrusts, a sudden rush and you forgot your family, your home. Sweet music swelled in your head as he whisked you away. Captured, you became his awesome, melodious voice while his eyes searched for the next prize.

II.
You were Rhea's secret child, Zeus's nameless sister, whom no one knew existed. Destined to live on earth, you begged for omniscience and a throne. For eons you sat alone gazing into what mortals call the unknown. The future was never a mystery— you always knew who was approaching long before they arrived and who lived, who died. Only two answers were never shown— your final destiny and where happiness is. Discontent being dreaded and revered, you wept each time a wedding party passed beneath your walless prison. What would you give to be like your brothers and sisters above, who in spite of their powers were all too human?

Crow Matinee

A lone crow squawked and cawed so much
he caught my after lunch inattention

while he arrowed to the ground,
swiped an empty ice cream cone

carrying it high into a bare tree.
As though he held a microphone,

his ruckus grew until another crow appeared.
The caucus balanced their empty cup on a limb,

examined it as though it were a cornucopia
passing it back and forth between them.

So much like politicians in their sleek, black suits.
Who knows what lies were told, promises made?

Finally, in agreement, they began feasting.
I smiled inside out at such craftiness:

their chiseled beaks' precision,
how they swallowed smidgens

never dropping one bit until the cone was gone.
Frost's words still echo inside my head,

"The way a crow shook down on me..."

Hop's Hammer Toes

That's what she called her crooked toes
with knots like a hammer's head
the way I nicknamed my great aunt *Hop*,
short for *Hopkins*.

Whenever Mother ran the vacuum cleaner,
we'd hide in her bedroom upstairs, door closed.
We hated noise like that and barking dogs
 but not cats; they were quiet.

Hop read me stories while I operated on her feet,
my five-year-old fingers working to make them straight.
"Behave toes," I'd speak as I stretched each one out,
then I'd frown as it curled back into the letter *c*.

This ritual was our way of coping with commotion:
people always moving in and out as though home
were a halfway house for misplaced lives:
aunts, uncles, cousins, neighbors in need,
faces and voices with eyes I did not trust.
Hop was my guardian from the unknown.

"Now listen to me," she'd repeat often. "Remember
to hold your head up high, your shoulders back,
and don't smile too much. Sensible people just don't
go around smiling. Act dignified." I tried.

Whenever I showed impatience with her unruly toes,
she'd tell me, "It's enough you keep trying.
That's how some things are — never just right.
Good always comes of effort, though."

Grown now, I sit alone, not smiling, wishing for her company.
"Hop, I'm really trying hard, but I'm losing my will.
Things like love and hammer toes seem impossible still."

War

> *in loving memory of Butch*

We played cowboy and Indian
on piles of lumber stacked in Grandma's yard.
For a while my long legs pogoed me over
plank after plank faster than you could anticipate
which way I'd go. Hiding was natural for me,
but sooner or later, I'd have to slow down.
You learned to find me by standing still.
"Bang, bang; you're dead," you'd say.
Dying was easy; I never felt a thing.
"Now see if you can catch me," you'd laugh and disappear.

Grandma tried to bribe you to stay out of Vietnam,
but you were a proud marine. "I'm not afraid," you smiled,
hugged me tight. I tried not to think of you
crouching in trenches, still. When you came home,
the part of you that laughed was gone. You sighed
and showed me pictures of dead children.
"I can't forget," is all you said, and kept your back to walls.

War followed you into a fading marriage you couldn't fake;
into middle age— double-crossed into a forced job loss.
Surrounded by enemies, you finally surrendered your will.
When I got the call that said you'd put a gun to your head,
all of those imaginary bullets exploded in my heart,
Bang, bang.

Aphrodisiac

In Poland on nights of a red moon,
they say women stir anisette and rum,
their blood flowing hot. Imagine
an old husband drinking the sweet potion—
his eyes glazed staring at her cleavage
as she leans over, edging closer. Sweat
beads on his forehead, and she
can feel heat rising from his body.
He reaches out his hand to touch her
somewhere. She refills his glass.

Shadow Boxing

Tabby cat tiptoes along a green metal fence before he jumps down
and sprints to the pool. Peering into the blue, he is not fooled
one second by his mirrored image, dips one paw and licks it.
Meanwhile, he has spied a lone bird soaring over sweet gums;
he freezes believing he can outwit it with cat-eye magic.

Unlike him, I'm not in touch with my innate powers.
Beside me an artificial fountain gurgles
as I struggle with words, phrases. They crash and scatter
like pick-up sticks onto page after page.
I cower at the voice in my head, "Give up! Hit delete."

Old trickster fear cuffs me in a ring that's closing in.
With every blow, he knocks the breath out of me.
It's no longer a question of win or lose; rather,
how much more I'll take before I awake to pack
a hit that means death to this faithful enemy.

I look into a mirror and shout, "Come out!"
I cannot be fooled by what I see.

Circusville

Years ago quite by accident, a circus grew in a small town.
Trainers, husband and wife, got bored with animals
so cracked whips at humans easy to teach tricks.
The master had his wife trained, too; but when he died,
she took his whip and outdid him. Easy enough,

her meek mother became a sweet, compliant seal
that balanced housework on her nose, cooking and cleaning
before she was allowed to eat. The mother barked ever so meekly
and never waddled in deep matters.

The nephew, smart but meek also, wore a clown's attire—
a solemn mask and a polka dot tie.
Since he was good at swallowing things,
auntie taught him to eat fire without choking.
Words were all it took, not one crack or mean look.
While he never objected out loud,
smoke poured from his ears. Once sleepwalking, he choked on it
and fumes drugged his senses. He wandered from home lost in a fog

until from out of nowhere, a fat lady appeared and captured him.
Married to her, he fell to despair as she lip-whipped hubby.
However, his mother, a wise fortuneteller foresaw her son's awakening.
This same clever lady resisted her sister,
who tried to bribe and tame her.

Circusville survived until the day the trainer's monkey disappeared.
Without his love to console her, she lost the will to control,
withdrew to her velvet lined trailer, and refused to come out.
Soon everyone quit their acts and the circus vanished,
though it's somewhere else no doubt.

Passing Time

She cannot see cracks in the ceiling, rotting boards in the floor,
or hear outside bulldozers roar, the hammers smack on steel.
All that is real are daily routines, patterns learned to survive
the fast-changing outside. On this newly-tarred road
where the schoolhouse once stood, large brick faces glare
at her peeling frame house. Still, Sarah will not leave home.

"Never have, never will," she declares staring
at something I cannot see.
"There's work to be done: the garden tended, grass mowed,
 beds weeded, pears picked before the blackbirds get them.
And this fall's apple crop, thick as ticks on a stray hound.
You watch. Early frost means a hard winter."

If I visit too long, she hums off- key, "Rock of Ages, Cleft for Me,"
as she rocks harder and gazes through a dusty window
at pale children whispering, chanting, whirling faster and faster
before the sound of the bell calls.

Like a Slow Anthrax

> *The bodies of a Roanoke woman and a Massachusetts man were delivered Friday to hospitals in Michigan by Dr. Jack Kevorkian. (The Roanoke Times, March 7, 1998)*

You never know where he'll strike next,
that infamous medical wonder, Dr. Death,

dropping off another victim somewhere:
unexpected gift wrapped in a body bag.

He's a wicked stork who delivers death
instead of birth when no one is expecting.

Can anyone believe that mercy
prompts him to offer an easy end?

Perhaps an evil force within guides his hand that slides
a needle deep into thin, withered skin.

Then an alien grin widens on him as it feeds
the need to destroy the human instinct to survive.

Spring Fever

Why not surrender to the invisible
energies wafting on spring's lazy wings—
angels' dust to slow us down long enough to learn
from daffodils or hyacinths what pleasures emerge during rebirth?

"Hurry up; get to work!" nags my itchy critic.
Instead of relaxing into sweet intoxication,
I coffee- and- chocolate myself to stay awake.
I stare at dimpled cement sidewalks
laden with cigarette butts, dried crusts of bread— human stuff.
Across the street a pocked, gray parking lot
is a shifting maze of rolling, colored boxes.

Shoulders taut, hands hawked over keys,
I berate myself, "Now write. Too late in life to dawdle."
It's the American way of life: rushpushurryup;
work day and night; make more money to spend faster—
unless, perhaps, I die in the process. Never mind.

I can't afford to wonder if I'll live long
into the wisdom of old age and look back in regret.
If I do, cover me with daffodils and hyacinths.
I'll have time to study from afar and learn how to reincarnate
as a guru in some remote place—
one who just sits, meditates, and watches life go by.

Auction

Louise stares at items displayed on her oak sideboard:
bone china teacups, pink depression dishes, a blonde Kewpie doll.

The beveled mirrored back doubles her confusion;
buzzing voices are gnats that nettle her nerves.

She wishes she could be like her husband was—
turn up the radio, tell them all to shut up. Instead, she clutches

a laced handkerchief tighter, dabs beads of sweat on her forehead;
sees pearl beads around the porcelain neck of the blue-eyed doll-child,

who becomes Louise laughing, squeezing a man's calloused hand.
As the Ferris wheel dips, he holds her tighter. She squeals.

"Nine hundred-once, twice– sold to number eleven!"
yells a big, bad man. Faces blur in spinning sun. Dizzy

she reaches into a half-opened drawer, takes out a faded paper, reads:
"The Secretary of War desires me to express his deep regret…"

Louise looks up at the wounded face in the mirror,
and behind it, the Ferris wheel whirling in the hazy light.

Lasting

In loving memory of Uno Kittee

Winter-toasted leaves are copper earrings dangling
from elephant-skin tree limbs glazed with snow.
Late February clipper made a quick pit stop in the dim hours of dawn.
Dream creatures scamper from my brain as in semi-sleepiness
my feet lead me across shiny hardwood floors and downstairs

where my old cat Romeo meows for Fancy Feast. Coffee in hand,
I walk through the backyard to fill a bird feeder
beside his brother Uno's new, muddy grave.
I am starving in more ways than one but cannot feed myself:
not even tender slices of milky sky or snow-iced pine cones.
Nothing known on earth appeases the hunger death creates.

I buried his remains in our new back yard he enjoyed
only three months— next to the gazebo, at the fence
where Uno met a gray- striped feline friend.
In sudden rain and sleet I strained to shovel heavy mud
enough to cover the cardboard casket that held his skinny remains.
Still cold and numb for days after, I wander through tasks
for grief is dumb— can neither count numbers nor tell time.
It only remembers to show up, fill you with pain, and linger.

I try to hold on to the good— especially those moments at the vet's
after Uno took his last breath and sent me a sign. Sitting in my car
outside, I looked up into the sky and saw him ascending backwards:
blue eyes staring into mine as thick, feathery wings lifted him quickly
out of sight. How typical of both God and Uno's love.

Off Season

Driving to the beach in September, I stop at the Planter's store
to squirrel nuts for winter: almonds, cashews, honey-roasted peanuts
brown- bagged, forbidden fat. The owner, a well-seasoned nut himself,
coaxes me with a corny joke: "How many days of a week begin with a
T? Four—Tuesday, Thursday, today, and tomorrow," he chuckles.

Just inside the beach front room, a sudden storm.
I lie beneath a skylight where lightning recharges me
and think of *Frankenstein*, his lonely monster. Tomorrow
I'll walk many sand miles and let the sea grandmother me.

Two days of rest, peace. The last night is moon full, icy white.
I roam the beach alone in the sweetness
of waves swishing and darkness.
My inner child wants to hide under a pier
hoping morning won't find us.

Dawn comes with heavy rain to ease my departure,
and I smile remembering the Planter's store owner's promise
of a new joke when I return.

The Visit

Doctor says she needs two surgeries, bladder and knees,
but does not guarantee that at eighty-eight, she'd wake up
to see spring's first daffodil open like a sudden yawn.

All night long she rolls, yawns, cannot sleep.
When dawn sprawls the horizon, she dreams
of falling down a hill, rolling, rolling until
Queenie dog grabs her coattail, drags her back.

Awake she snails herself out of bed and
canes her way down five steps to the bay
window, where she squints to see if a yellow head
has risen yet from the emerald lawn. Instead,

swaying down the sidewalk two familiar heads:
the curly blonde waves a bottle of Old Crow,
the tall brunette's arm shawled over his brother's shoulders.

"Dear Lord!" It's her brothers Sam and George
grinning, singing, "When the Roll is Called Up Yonder."
"Wonder if they've been working the graveyard shift?
So like those two rascals not to call ahead."

A thrust of energy rushes her to the kitchen
where she brews strong coffee, reaches to the top shelf
for their stained, white mugs and Mama's blue china cup.

"God bless those two rascals!" she chuckles as she rushes
to unlock the front door. After long hugs, she'll fuss
at them for dying, leaving her to carry on alone.

Guess they didn't know she'd live so long
until all her childhood friends were gone.
She always was the strongest one.

Verbal Convolution

Another mopey Saturday in this sluggish city,
another cup of bitter Verona at B and N Café.
Caffeine and sugar chatter statics the air:
a muddle of dreams and troubles that makes me
stare at the blank computer screen.

Sister calls my cell phone and says I must swear
not to tell anyone good news she has for me, and so it is.
Uncommon peace eases me; noise becomes harmony.
I exhale and feel my cellophane shroud crinkle loose.

Then it happens as usual— a tightening in my throat
alerts me this won't last; we're not alone.
Tongue-tying demon rises from a den of mistrust
lodged inside us since childhood.
Gnarled fingers snatch up sentences,
split them apart, and spit them out.
Hard words hurl through the air
and stone us into a blue-black silence.

I hang up the phone. Demon is gone,
but a chorus of mad rappers cracks open my head,
blows smoke in my face. I cough,
choking as they mock me:

"Your mother's shrinking; her house caving in.
Your daddy's still crying from his grave.
Your sister's grasping for life given away.
You better save them before it's too late."

Jamestown Ferry Ride

Just in time at the dock to catch the six o'clock sunset,
my friend Betty guides her Lincoln over the deck to the front row
while I stare at bold stripes of rusty orange, thin gold ones,
the salmon glow. We spring onto the bow greeted by
a sobering 40-degree air. We laugh, don't care

that wind whips our hair as Pocahontas snakes through the water.
We're floating in a cup rimmed by a dark band
of trees on distant shores.
We snap pictures as though we can capture pleasure.
Smothered too long by civilization, I feel an urge to be bold,
strip off my clothes, dive in, revive myself.

Too soon we spot pilings topped with sea gulls,
hear their squeaky-squawky talk of our approach.
I wrap my coat tighter around me, breathe deeply,
soak this scene into my pores.

As we land at the Jamestown settlement site,
history vies for my attention until I remember
this is it.

Java and Jive

I sip Butter Rum coffee listening
to soft soprano, Celtic bagpipes and violins
blend with the coffee grinder's slippery whisper.

A young man in a brown suede coat
sways in past round tables to the bar.
He could be a movie star or some woman's
hand-fed, secret lover. He winks at me.
I grin and wonder if I should know him.

Last night I danced and danced tango, rumba, samba;
yet, it's single-time swing that ignites me
like a triple shot of steamy, hot espresso.

My best partner is an angel with broad wings,
so light on his feet it's hard to know he's there.
I never know when he'll appear
so while I'm dancing with a good partner,
I discreetly pinch him on the back of his arms.

At the Same Time

I.

Her bones are so filled with dried hay left in the fields since her son went away that her steps make no impression on the hard road ahead: ruts she follows, deep lines on the face in her mirror. Knotted hands reach for a faded, yellow ribbon tied around the mailbox, smoothing each satin curl of his hair before she removes a letter and holds it close to her eyes. A passing car blows its horn, slows down, but she doesn't hear or see it slide into a ditch. Nothing exists but the letter in one hand tucked in her pocket.

Inside the house she pokes hickory sticks into the fire, pours hot water from a kettle for her usual tea. Now in the rocking chair, she opens his letter and savors scrawled lines until she knows them by heart. Late afternoon sun casts an anesthetic shadow over her as she prays. A few pieces of tea leaves swirl in pale liquid; sizzling from the wood grows faint. By sunset the leaves are as still as the woman who sleeps by the dying fire.

II.

Seeing a woman ahead, I slow down to ponder the yellow ribbon she caresses when a young buck leaps in front of me. My car veers to the right. I hit the horn and brake, sliding into a shallow ditch. Fear, shock; time stops. Will the deer's small rack smash the glass window in my face as my torso thrusts forth and back against the seat? Will our wild eyes meet with our last breaths while death grapples with our spirits, snatches them up? Or will the deer be quick and leap aside to safety as death speeds to another scene, and I'm left shocked but unhurt?

Continued...

III.

In Iraq a young American soldier dazed by a crimson-yellow sunset
pauses behind a building only seconds more than the rest of his
squad. Frozen there, he is spared a spray of gunfire that forks the flesh
of comrades, their blood red-washing the foreign street.
His best buddy sprawls just feet away, and horrified eyes stare
up into his— a look he will never outlive.

Fall's Lure

Distant Blue Ridge Mountains roller coaster
over ice blue skies dolloped with white clouds.

Trees have shed bland, green uniforms— peaks wild with color:
red romance, yellow and orange fire— all wine for my spirits.

This morning I'm filled with something between desire and hunger
as I wonder what secrets mountains hold in their stony hearts

of those who disappeared there— ghosts wandering
winding trails, lurking in abandoned shacks. Some

bored or lonely cast spells on sleeping campers,
slip into their skin, follow them home. One such man

could not explain eerie changes— his dog's fear of him,
an aversion to mirrors, the urge to wander outside at night.

Late afternoon cobalt shadows ribbon giant slopes;
sun spotlights trees. As I move a live kaleidoscope follows me.

My heart so inspired wants to flee into these hills
and live with mysteries that defy reality.

Market Street Blues

On a bench in front of the theater,
he plays harmonica, tin cup wedged between his knees,
feet tapping the rapid beat.
When he smiles with his eyes, I follow
deep lines in his dark face, a maze
that leads to some ancient secret.
Beside him a blonde man in jeans joins in, trumpet crooning.

Soon blues writhes its way through the coffee shop door,
circles the floor, sniffing like a coon dog
before it decides to linger and mingle
with the cash register's chit-chit-zing,
the spoons' clinking in cups,
and the cappuccino machine's hisses.
Human words swarm for space
as the line of customers grows.

Outside a girl and boy entwine and kiss,
their purple and orange hair blending
with vendors' bronze and yellow mums,
red apples, and the small suns of sweet potatoes.
.
Harmonica man looks around and nods
as though he's satisfied it's good.
I think of God and expect a miracle:
the corner artist's carved, wooden menagerie
of elephants, lions, tigers will rise up alive
and walk through these streets in and out of stores,
tame and unnoticed.

On the Chesapeake Bay

Wrapped in pines that wind around the bay,
Ray and I lounge on his screened-in porch,
sip green tea, and inhale hot August morning air.
I watch the water as he explains how bait fish jump up
and the rock fish slaps its tails on the surface.

A blue Johnboat holding a woman and two boys
drifts silently into the cove and out of sight—
just the way dreams slide through sleeping brains.

Who knows? Maybe Dennis, dozing next door,
dreamed this scene before the eternal current
carried all such musings to a place where nothing lies
between your skin and mine and the totality of existence.

Champions

They flow, swirl, wind apart then back together again and again.
Her red silk skirt flutters, flirting with his sleek, black tights.

Once he slips, falls and scoops himself up— magnificent accident.
Puppet on string, she never flinches or misses a beat
although her nerves are fireworks her heart stops to watch.

He glides to her side, and they dance so solo-duo
that woman, man, music merge. Finally,
he twirls her into the air where she spins
to land entwined with him.

Baucis and Philemon
carved on ice.

For Men Only

In our pocketbooks
we women carry dreams
and things invisible to men.
I keep a pool of cheese and blue wine
in the bottom of mine.
In a secret part
an inflatable lover lies.

My billfold is always heavy
ready with changes of moods and disguises.
Blazing fingernails crawl from the seams.
Handles are ready whips.

When I open my pocketbook wide
unleash a red unicorn
who rides me on the winds.
He knows where I'm going.

Part 3

Power Play

Cast

Madeleine (Maddie): A stylish, attractive woman

Reynaldo: An attractive man around 40

Wise Woman: An older woman

Fat Fiends: In costumes to depict their names

Men and Women: Various ages, ethnicities

Act I

Scene 1: *The stage is bare and lights dim. The four veils hang closer to the middle of the stage. Loud, ominous sounds (sirens, alarms, gun fire, screams) can be heard intermittently. Shadows of people are seen moving. Enter a man dressed in black from stage left who wanders through the veils as if lost and frightened. His head hangs down, and he refuses to look up. He glances anxiously behind him, sometimes stumbling. Enter stage right a woman also dressed in black. She mimics his actions. They wander in and out of the veils until they bump into each other, and she screams and backs away. All appear to dance in a free style as though chasing each other. The music intensifies, and their movement becomes more frantic. The man beckons for the young woman to come with him as he pushes forward out of the veils. She refuses. He stands looking after her. From down one aisle Wise Woman walks carrying a flashlight and wearing a gold hat. Calmly and slowly, she moves up onto the stage, where she pauses and watches the fiasco looking concerned and shaking her head. She then points her flashlight onto the first man who stops and walks in slow motion toward her. As he approaches center front stage, the others move behind the veils one by one and the music fades. The man and Wise Woman stand center stage with a spotlight on them. His head is still down. As Wise Woman speaks to him and the audience, he raises his head little by little.*

Wise Woman: Fear *(emphasizing the word loudly)* is nothing but a fake thought that somebody scarder than you stuck up in your head like a wad of Juicy Fruit gum. Now, I'm a believer, so may I remind you that the good Lord won't no deceiver when he said we are children created in His Holy image, which does not conjure up no idea of fear. Come to think of it, God didn't prefer snakes, but nowhere in the Bible does it say he ran from or killed any. No indeed, not even that sly one that messed up the first and last and best garden party that God threw for us. Now that you understand that where I'm coming from, erect your spines in them seats and let the light of Truth shine in! We must respect all God's creatures (at a respectable distance, of course.) Which is to say plainly, *Thou shall not kill—* not even a snake— because the Word says it's the respectable thing to do. However, it does not disallow removing yourself from its ugly presence to do some hard, fast praying that the Almighty will remove all fear from you and also the snake, too, at the same time— if not sooner.

(She takes off her gold hat and places it on the man's head. Then she hands him the flashlight and exits stage right.) The man looks up, smiles, stands tall and dances around until the ominous music starts again, and the characters behind the curtain move as before. The man in the gold hat goes confidently into the midst of them searching. He sees the same woman fighting a shadow until she falls to her knees. He grabs her hand. She resists, but he manages to fight their way through the others and to the front stage. The music stops and the people behind the veils freeze).
Woman: Leave me alone! Who are you? What do you want? *(She looks at the man and glances around frantically and tries to run. He runs after her and tries to block her.)*
Man: Please wait! Calm down. I'm only trying to help you.
Woman: Help! Help! *(She screams and runs back into the shadows. Voices scream; guns shots; one shadow falls; sirens sound. The man stands a moment looking after her and goes back into the shadows.)*
Blackout

Scene 2: *Four veils hang from the ceiling as a backdrop. Stage left has a door. Stage right holds a coat rack with a metallic gold hat on it. A dim spotlight shines on it.*

Reynaldo: Well, hello there. I'm the studio owner, Reynaldo. Just call me Rey. So what's your name?
Maddie: It's nice to meet you. I'm Madeleine, and you may call me Maddie.
Reynaldo: Delighted to meet you, Maddie. What a nice dress. So, you like dancing?
Maddie: Thank you. Yes. I like what little I know, but I want to learn more.
Reynaldo: That's great. I'm not busy at the moment, so let's take a spin around the floor so I can tell what to recommend. What's your favorite dance?

Maddie: Swing, without a doubt. It makes me happy. (*He starts the music, takes her hand and leads her to the floor. Maddie is reluctant at first but follows him in a simple swing.*)
Reynaldo: (*smiling*) Lady, you're a natural! Great sense of rhythm! We'll be on "Dancing with the Stars" before you know it.
Maddie: Thanks, but I doubt that. I think you are the one making it easy. I just want to learn enough to feel as though I know what I'm doing and to have fun.
Reynaldo: Give yourself some credit. Now you know the saying, "It takes two to tango." So we'll focus our lessons with rhythm dances and throw in smooth for variety. Your build is perfect for smooth. (*He looks at her and grins. Music switches to a tango. He pulls her close and begins to dance.*)
Maddie: Isn't this too close? I can barely move.
Reyaldo: No indeed. You have to feel my lead. (*Maddie manages to follow awkwardly. Music stops, and he continues to hold her a little too long. She pulls away obviously a bit shaken. He smiles.*)
Reynaldo: How did you like that, Isadora? That is your middle name, right? You've got a good sense of rhythm and you're easy to lead. Let's go over here and take a look at my book. (*He takes her hand and leads her to the sofa. Maddie sits to catch her breath while Reynaldo gets her glass of water. He looks at her with a big smile.*) So, are you free during the day so we can start getting serious (*grinning at her*) about dance?
Maddie: Not much at all really. I work very long hours and sometimes travel without much notice. I'm the manager, which means I have more to do. Early evening is best for me.
Reynaldo: Okay. I can arrange that. No problem. Could weekends be free, too, I hope?
Maddie: Maybe some. It all depends on the business. (*Lights fade and Maddie walks to one end of the stage and Reynaldo the other. Spotlight shines on him.*)
Reynaldo: Um! Does she look good— sexy but not a one-night stand. Real classy! This may not be as easy as usual. Wonder what she thinks of me? She's hard to read. Teaching her anything will sure make work seem like fun for a change, but I'll have to be careful. This one may be worth my time. She has a good job and is the boss, too.
Maddie: Boy! Is he forward, or am I imaging it? What in the world is going on? This chemistry I feel with him is scary. I thought I was

too old for this, and he is not at all my type. I don't know whether I should run or stay. I think I've been without a date too long. He's good looking and has enough charisma to charm Medusa. Part of me wants to run, and part wants to stay. I'm really off balance! *(They freeze and the spotlight fades. A purple light follows Wise Woman as she walks across and stops center stage wearing a gold hat. She addresses both the couple and the audience.)*

Wise Woman: When the tentacles of temptation tackle you in the most ticklish parts of your physiology, and without apology, ain't but one or two things you can do that will do you any good. And that don't mean doing what you want to do without thinking about where you want to end up. Now, some say listen to your heart and some say heed your head. I say the good Lord gave you both of them parts to use together— providing one of them ain't dead. But watch out for the third part at the other end! It's got a will of its own much stronger than it is longer or wide, and it will lead you to illusions of confusion. In fact, there ought to be a bumper sticker that says, "Just Say No to Your Libido!" Unless, of course, you are hitched for life to another, and then you should not have no other under any cover.

(**Wise Woman** *continuing*) And there's plenty more snares that lead to despair. There's the gremlin of gluttony and the tempest of tongues, both which issues from out your mouth. I say somebody with some science sense should commence to inventing a micro-chip that would zip up lips to keep something bad from coming or going through them. Then there's the noose of negativity that hangs around folks' necks and chokes every idea they get. There ought to be a law against saying, *I can't*, because that's far worse than any drug. It paralyzes your brain with fear till your gears get locked up, and you ain't going nowhere. Then there's the mobster-lobster teaser, gambling, which is by far the worse of the curses attached to purses. You get the fever so bad that not even Madonna dressed as a nurse could get you to stop rolling craps or slapping at Black Jack or reeling over a roulette wheel. So I say, children of the Almighty that we are to refrain from all such temptations that control your souls and lead to your ruination!
Blackout

Scene 3: *(When lights go back up, Wise Woman is gone. Maddie and Reynaldo are in the center front practicing a cha cha. No music)*

Reynaldo: Remember to lean forward. Stay on the balls of your feet. That's it. Just listen the beat— one, two, cha, cha, cha. Nice. Small steps. Shoulders down, please. Tuck in your middle; it's your control for everything (*He presses her abdomen.*) Much better. Now get ready for a double spin. Remember to spot me.
Maddie: (*Maddie stumbles on the second turn, pulls away suddenly and stops.*) Shoot! I can't remember the steps. What's wrong with me? This is too frustrating! Can we just skip this one for now? I've had a hard day at work, and this is not helping my stress.
Reynaldo: No. You're not a quitter. Just relax and follow me, Baby. Don't look down. Just follow me. Think about how good we're going to look in that competition in a couple of months. You're doing great. We've only been practicing a few weeks. Just relax and let me lead. That's my job here, you know. Why don't you think about our wonderful date last night?
Maddie: (*smiling*) Maybe that's the problem. I was dancing better before. I assure you there won't be any competition for me unless I feel a lot better about my dancing than I do now. If I'm going to compete, Rey, I'm going to know I'm ready. I'm not one to make a fool of myself on purpose.
Reynaldo: Don't' worry, Maddie. You will be ready. I promise. You have to learn to trust me. I know a winner when I see one. You just need to relax. Remember— it's muscle memory. Once you get it, you've got it. Now let's switch to …
Maddie: Well, I know I'm too tired to concentrate, Rey. I need a break. My muscles couldn't remember right from left at this point. (*A young woman enters and stands just inside the doorway. Rey turns away quickly from Maddie and glances nervously at the woman.*)
Reynaldo: Excuse me a minute. I'll be right back. Practice your Cuban motion for me. I like to watch those hips. (*Maddie practices while he and a woman talk. At first the woman smiles and then looks annoyed. Rey follows her outside the door. Reynaldo returns to Maddie putting his hands on her hips as though to lead her.*)
Maddie: Is everything okay?

Reynaldo: No. Yes. It was just somebody at the wrong place. Let's finish this one routine and we'll quit. (*He tries to continue the lesson, but he glances at the door and keeps making mistakes.*) Sorry, Baby. I've got a headache. Let's stop for now. Okay?
Maddie: Oh, I'm sorry, but that's fine with me. We are still going out tonight, right? At seven? Do you think you'll feel like it?
Reynaldo: Of course we are. I'll just take a quick nap or something. (*He blows her a kiss.*) Wear something sexy just for me. Okay?
Maddie: Who are you talking to, Rey? That is disrespectful. You know I'm not like that. I don't buy into society's obsessions with sex!
Reynaldo: Calm down. I was just kidding, Baby. I wanted to see if you were paying attention. Don't take everything so serious. I am a man, you know.
Maddie: Yes. And remember, I am a lady.
Reynaldo: Of course, Dear. (*He escorts her quickly to the door. Afterwards, he pulls out his cell phone and dials it.*) Hi. The lesson is over. I got rid of her early just for you, Baby. Come on over.
Lights fade.

Scene 3: *At one end of the front stage Maddie (dressed to go out) is at home where she sits in a chair writing in a journal and drinking a cup of coffee. She speaks out loud what she is writing.*

Maddie: Am I worrying too much? Rey is so much fun but also sometimes alarming. He makes me almost lose reason, and I don't like not being level-headed. Like good business, I know not to jump into anything, but this feels so good and I've been lonely so long. I just can't ignore the agitated feeling I get sometimes around him. I lose energy. I've always heard that when it's right, it's right, and you know it; I don't. I wish I'd get a clear sign if he's right for me.(*The phone rings, and Maddie picks it up.*) Hello. Rey? (*pause*) What? Tonight? No.Why didn't you call me sooner? Yes. I do realize you had a headache, but it's so late. You are supposed to be on the way. Yes I'm upset because I've worked hard to get this time off, and this is not the first time. Yes, you did. You cancelled on me once before for last minute business. Remember? No. I don't want to catch a virus. You could have called earlier. (*Maddie places the receiver down on the phone and speaks to herself.*)

I have a feeling he's not telling me the truth, but why wouldn't he? He's like Jeckel and Hyde! I knew something was not right about him, but I've lied to myself. I care about him, but I don't like his ways. I can't stand people who are unreliable. How can you build trust? Is it worth the trouble? But what if he really is sick?

(Lights fade on her and go up at the other back side of the stage where Reynaldo puts down the phone and goes to open the door to the woman who had visited the studio earlier. He smiles and embraces her. They freeze and lights go up at other end where Maddie stands pacing the floor. The Wise Woman enters and Maddie freezes.)

Wise Woman: Don't you know that indecision is an incision in your brain that runs through it like a big, fast, northbound train led backwards by a caboose driven by a mongoose? It keeps running 'til the ruts get deeper than the sleep of death itself; then you sink into the mire and lose all desire to be alive and awake. This is when you either wallow in the crud you created or get yourself a shovel and grovel your way out. Otherwise, you'll lay down and rot in your own sniveling snot and be buried alive and declared half-wise and covered by a shroud of flies. So listen up! The only solution is to ask God to call out His best-baked batch of angel guards with their biggest prods to poke you in the right direction. But don't think He'll make decisions for you because He won't meddle with the voice of your choice. He will, however, make some revision in your contorted vision of the whole situation. Then, Friends, you can decide how to stop the crazy train from tracking up your brain and normalize your equilibrium, so as: your liver no longer shivers and your teeth don't chiver-chatter and your bones don't rattle and your tongue don't tattle twisted tales into your ears. Instead of feeling like a sliver off a slab of rotten bologna, you'll soon be dancing a jig like a pig named Lucky that cut loose the noose just before he would've lost his juice to a big, bad butcher that was after his pink, plump, porkified rump.
Blackout

Act II

Scene 1: *When lights go up again, Maddie and Rey are in the studio. Rey is on the phone, which he takes far to a corner for privacy.*

Maddie: Rey, you seem disturbed lately. What's wrong?
Reynaldo: What do you mean? You're just imaging things.
Maddie: You just don't seem to be present with me.
Reynaldo: Oh, no. I didn't think you were one of those jealous, insecure women. I told you, nothing is wrong. You don't understand this business. If I don't cater to some of these wealthy clients, I'll lose them.
Maddie: I'm just concerned. I'm afraid it's more than business, Rey. Is there a problem with our relationship? Is there someone else?
Reynaldo: Are you trying to say I'm running around on you— the best catch in the city? I'd be a fool. No woman can compare with you. You know by now I'm crazy about you.
Maddie: I'm not accusing you; just asking why you act different, Rey. I'm a sensitive person, so I know when things don't feel right.
Reynaldo: I'll show you what feels right is. (*He pulls her to him kisses her passionately. Enter a young couple arguing and Reynaldo goes towards them.*)
Man: I told you this is stupid. We don't need to waltz to get married. We'll do the dancing on the honeymoon at clubs.
Woman: But you promised me we would waltz at our wedding, and you need to keep your word. You know it means a lot to me.
Man: I was just saying that to get you to say, "Yes." I never thought I really would have to dance. You know I've got two, maybe three left feet.
Woman: Well. You are about to lose them if you want to marry me. You shouldn't have lied about it. Always be honest. That is the most important thing in a relationship.
Reynaldo: (*To Maddie.*) Excuse me, but I've never seen these people before. Be right back. (*He rushes to greet the couple. Maddie stands in place looking perplexed.*)
Reynaldo: Hi, I'm Reynaldo, the studio owner. How may I help you?
Woman: We'd like to learn to waltz for our wedding in a month. Is that possible?

Man: No! *She* would like to, not me. Can it be done in one lesson, I hope?
Woman: Please just be quiet and let this man talk. Besides the wedding, dancing is good exercise, and you could use some.
Man: So is digging ditches, which is free. How much does this cost? You know the honeymoon is costing four thousand.
Woman: Money! Is that what is so important? I'm spending just as much on the wedding. You don't seem to worry about cost when it comes to beer and sports.
Man: Speaking of beer, I'm going to need lots if I have to fancy dance in front of people.
Woman: Well. Start stocking up because I'm not changing my mind.
Man: You may by the time I walk all over you.
Woman: What! Just how do you mean that?
Reynaldo: Excuse me. I think I can help. It's an easy dance—just making a box. You two are in luck today. Let me show you. My fiancée is here, and I'm teaching her a dance for our wedding. She didn't know how to either— awkward as could be. Now I want you to see what a miracle worker I am. Sit down and let us give you a little demonstration. (*Reynaldo goes to Maddie and talks. He pulls her to the couple.*) Just a minute. She's a little shy, folks.
Woman: (*to Maddie*) I see you've had better luck with your fiancée than I have.
Maddie: Fiancée? Oh, no. We're not engaged.
Reynaldo: (*Laughing nervously at the couple*). She's just mad at me right now.
Man: Yeah! I know what you mean. Excuse us. (*Rey pulls Maddie aside whispering*)
Maddie: Did you tell them we're getting married? That's dishonest! You haven't even mentioned marriage to me.
Reynaldo: Maybe I'm fantasizing, but please help me out here, Baby. Just play along, and let them see how good they could look. Don't you want to help me? No harm done.
Maddie: Why do you need to lie to them? That's not right. (*Rey turns on music and beckons Maddie out onto the dance floor. Maddie just stands still.*)

Reynaldo: Sorry, folks. *(He laughs nervously looking at the couple. Lights dim on both couples who freeze as Wise Woman enters and walks to center front stage. She looks at them and shakes her head.)*

Wise Woman: *Matrimony* sort of sounds like *bologna* which makes a very good sandwich; however, if you let it rot, it causes a worse case of trots than a group of galvanized gophers ganged up to pulverize your yard. Which is why the Lord laid it on my heart to set you straight from the start. First, only for you men here— grooms to be or wishing for it to be. On the sacred subject of sex. Don't put no hex on your honeymoon by going to the wrong places just because you too tight-fisted to go first class. Like don't take her to public libraries just because she likes to read, and don't' go to no zoos for observation of the sacred act of consummation. You know the sacred act comes after the wedding, which rhymes with shedding and bedding and speaks for itself. Being the lady I am, I'll only say only remember this: After the wedding, when the spirit moves you to shedding in the bedding, put a lid on you head so you don't accidentally produce any unwanted human produce. Men, I beg you this one time to hear the truth and cut yourself loose from the noose of chains which has your brains shackled to your lower parts. And now that all being said, we women need to *parle vous* about you.

(Men step back mechanically and women move forward— all still in trance-like position. They do not react to her words. Wise Woman addresses Maddie and the other woman.

Wise Woman: Sweet sisters! Listen for your lives. I have researched, selected and perfected secret rules of surviving and thriving in marriage— data that is matter tried and true by our foremothers, who weathered storms of long-lasting unions and won the wedded wars.

Rule number...
1. Pick a man like you would a horse—one with some spirit but what can be bridled and tamed to mind you.
2. You *got* to have three sets of dishes: one for eating; one for company; and one for throwing.

3. Always ask the preacher and your mother-in-law to dinner, and serve your man's favorite meal— just before you tell him you bought something expensive.
4. Last and most important is pray every day for the Lord to bless you both with the faith of Moses, the wisdom of Solomon, the strength of David, and the patience of Job.

Blackout.

Scene 2: *When the curtain opens, Reynaldo is dancing close with the first woman who had appeared at the studio. He whispers in her ear and they flirt. They are laughing and do not see Maddie appear and stand in doorway watching. Finally, he sees Maddie, and says something to the woman. The woman looks annoyed, gets her coat and goes out in a huff. Reynaldo approaches Maddie.*

Reynaldo: Baby, what are you doing here? I thought you had to work late. (*He tries to pull her to him, but she resists.*)

Maddie: Isn't that the same woman who was here "lost" a few weeks ago? It looks as though she found her way back.

Reynaldo: No. She's just a new client. I have to make sure she has a good time. You know how I have to play up to them. It just part of the business, Baby.

Maddie: I'm sure it is, but I think it must be part of you, too. Isn't that what you did with me, Rey? Play up to me at first to make me feel good? I'm not stupid. That is the same woman. Well, maybe she's more your type. (*She turns away to leave. He grabs her by the hand and kisses her and pulls her onto the dance floor. As they dance a passionate tango, Maddie's anger is visible. The Wise Woman in the gold hat appears and stands watching. As Maddie and Rey finish, a purple light leads Maddie to the hat rack. She picks up the hat and puts it on her head walking to the mirror. As she looks into it, the light gets brighter the veils go up. Background music "Blues in the Night." Maddie moves toward Rey and stands in front of him scowling with her hands on her hips. They freeze as Wise Woman speaks.*)

Wise Woman: After I gave you the best first-class love this side of heaven, you slithered around like a wicked, wall-eyed weasel, a low-class, mean-ass, spineless beast who's about to take a licking for picking on the wrong woman that you, in your evilized state of sordid

sinfulness, mistook for another sleek-meek-weak, easy-to-cheat chicken. *(Veils rise slowly as Maddie continues, her voice getting louder and stronger.)* Now I bet you thought I'd roll over, scratch the dirt, and come crawling and bawling for crumbs of mercy. Well, the good Lord have mercy on your shriveled soul, old boy! You just swallowed your last bad breath of devil's work because Maddie has called forth the powers of the Salvation Sisters, bound in blood and sworn to the Angel of Mercy to protect all women molested by any size heart-breaking-no-giving-all-taking womanizer! We specialize in resizing fat baloney butts like yours with our Shriveling Sensation Number! It recycles all parts of any male loser-boozer-users like you till we make something worth letting loose. We guarantee to wipe any trace of smirk off your phony face, strip down your false pride, and force you to face the Almighty with your naked shame lightening up your dark soul. You'll feel like the last tail feather of the sickest chicken plucked in slow motion, skinned and fried alive for Fourth of July Sunday dinner. When the Salvation Sisters are through humanizing your soul, your head will be reeling, your voice squealing for the chance to beg forgiveness from this sweet mama of mercy, the champion of broken-hearted females, the one and only amazing, gracious Maddie, who will never again let any man around get this woman down! *(Maddie has backed Rey off of the stage and both disappear.)*
Curtain

Act III

Scene 1: *Noises are heard behind the curtain—screams, sirens, ambulance, gunshots. The stage is dim. A man chasing another with a gun runs from center curtain. The same frightened woman from the beginning runs across the stage towards the first man who had tried to help as he enters from the opposite end. She bumps into him and turns around to run. He grabs her hand.*

Man: Wait! Please! I've been looking for you. Please just talk to me.
Woman: No! I told you to leave me alone! (*As she pulls away, a drunk stumbles from center and reaches for her. The first man intervenes and gets the drunk out of the way. The woman watches and then runs the opposite way.*)
Man: No! Don't go back. I want to help you.
Woman: Yeah! Right! Just like everyone else. (*She runs toward the shadows. He stands a moment and then runs after her back into the shadows. The same ominous noises occur*).
Blackout

Scene 2: *The stage is bare except for a semi-circle of chairs in the center and a coat rack. Light shines on it where Maddie sits in front of a group of women and one man varying in ages and ethnicities. Maddie, wearing a gold hat, addresses the women. Wise Woman sits in back row by herself and unseen.*

Maddie: I've told you most of my story. Once I realized I do not have to be a victim of anybody, I felt a surge of energy that has never left me. The important things are not what happens but what we learn during those times. It's the same for all of us. Ladies, we were never meant to hate men, but to choose carefully. The same is true for men. I ask you to consider this: would you choose to live in a run-down or badly constructed house? Would you buy a house or car without checking it out thoroughly and inspecting it? Now, who else in here has been enlightened and has something to share? (*A young woman waves her hand, stands, and speaks.*)
Woman 1: Once I saw the truth, I got rid of my boyfriend, but I'm going through a long, hard time of being afraid alone. I had to have something to do or I'd go crazy.

Woman 2: I'm right there with you. I just broke up with my boyfriend, and all I can do is cry and shop or eat and drink. How long am I supposed to wait to date?

Woman 3: Yeah, well. I'm not about to wait, sit home and grow old alone. Time flies and men are scarce. There's nothing wrong with just going out with men for company. If I want a man, I want one when I want one. I'm online dating with two sites.

Woman 1: How's that working for you? I'm scared of those things.

Woman 3: Well. It beats sitting at home, but you kiss a lot of frogs with warts.

Woman 1: So have you met anyone special?

Woman 3: No. But I'm not sitting home alone.

Maddie: I'm not trying to tell anyone what to do when I'm just sharing what I learned. Right after anything serious involving our emotions, it takes a while to process them and think clearly—especially if it meant a lot to you. You've heard the saying, "Out of the frying pan and into the fire." I don't think people do that on purpose. You won't die being alone; in fact, you'll learn a lot. Take some classes; work on hobbies. It's like discovering a new person. Give yourself a year to get clear, and I bet you won't regret it. Then after that... (*As she is finishing these lines, Wise Woman stands up and moves the front. The group freezes. Light fades on group and up on Wise Woman.*)

Wise Woman: After the mourning time has passed and the angst of anger over wasted days and nights of unnatural agony; and especially after you done laid low that pork-headed, mud-slopping, no-stopping, tight-lipped womanizing-miser and turned over what's left of him to the Savior of all times: then and only then is what I'm posed to tell you is the sure way to purify and securify your sweet souls. First, shake off your mourning clothes and put on a fancy, red dress and some classy high heel shoes. Strut your most elegant self around town like a crowned queen. Let out the vibes that you have arrived; however, be careful in the selection of any object of your affection. Choose a few good men to wine and dine you. Pick the ever so lean in limbs but rich in heart men. Get the ones who can stand up alone on their own and not looking to pick your bones. Spare rest to shop for the best, and be careful to go slow 'til you know he ain't up to a quick ego fix.

(*Pause. As she is speaking, a group of men come by and she looks them over and orders them away*).

Wise Woman (*continuing*): Many men are wonderful to behold like a mountain of gold as well as great to hold and be held by— especially when they let you cry on them strong shoulders that act like boulders to hold you up when the tides of life roll you down and over. Now we women are more soft like fine cloth, and soft needs hard like a frying pan needs lard to cook up anything good. I don't know about you, but I like a good man to cook for, to cook with, and to look at, look over and so forth. I mean solo is not so grand as one fine man because what a woman can do with one is far more fun than without— without a doubt. (*Enter a well-dressed man who approaches her, and she puts her arm in his smiling as she looks him over.*)

Wise Woman (*continuing*): What I'm proposing in closing is that if you find a real good man, you best hang on tight as you can— because if you turn him loose, someone else will tuck him up fast and tight like her papoose. In short, don't be like the dumb gander that had found a grand goose but then spied a cute, red caboose on the loose and chased it 'till she fell on her face and broke her honker and lost both males and never could even tell her sad tale. (*Lights fade on her as she sits down and back up on the group.*)

Maddie: We need to be careful not to knock all men just because a few have been rotten to us, because even with them, we had lessons to learn. While they burned us like brine on a cut, it is all in the grand design. Besides some women do the same thing to men. Right, friends? (*They nod in agreement and turn toward the one man in the group.*)

Maddie: Ladies, let's turn our attention to our friend, our faithful, brave one man in our group. How's your situation, friend? We're so glad you're here again.

Man: (*hesitates*) I don't know what to say.

Maddie: Oh? Did we scare you with all our talk, or are you confused?

Man: (*looks down and mumbles*) He shakes his head, "No."

Maddie: Good. Will you share a little, please? Keeping all this locked inside will make you sick. We know you've been going through a hard time. How is at home?

Man: Worse. I feel like killing her, not saying I would.

Maddie: Well. I know you are smarter than that, which is why you are here. Have you convinced her you want a divorce?
Man: No. I've tried a long time, but she won't budge. She just threatens me. We yell and fight, but I won't give up. I just don't know what else to do.
Women: That's right! Stand your ground.
Maddie: There is a way out. I think you are almost there. It's a test. I bet you are stronger than you realize, friend.
(*Wise woman gets up, goes to him and places the gold hat on his head. A purple light shines on him. Slowly he straightens himself up, rises from his seat and speaks.*)
Man: I'm sick of that woman controlling me. I'm sick of her nagging and whining. As a matter of fact, I'm sick of everything about her! I give and give and she takes and takes. There's nothing in it for me. It's not worth it. I feel worse than a door mat— I feel like the dirt ground into it. (*Freeze except for Wise Woman who speaks.*)
Wise Woman: Hen pecked men, get ready to be roosterfied. Put some spine in your head and tell that wicked, wide-mouth wench to get a grip on her out-of-control ego and leave her to nag herself into a coma. The main problem is that you not trusting your own God-given power to know that you know what's right for you. Instead you are glued to the notion that somebody louder or bolder or younger or older knows better. That's a cop-out and drop-out from living your tailor-made life. We all been born with instincts and brains to make us the only decoder of our own book of instructions called, *This Is My Life*. No wife can understand the grand plan that comes through God's hands and into our souls if we hold still long enough to behold it. I tell you, every bone has got to stand alone on his own or be crushed to dust in the fuss and rush gushing from others. (*She returns to her seat and the group resumes*)
Man: (*standing and smiling*) All of a sudden I feel... what is it? Alive— full of energy. He smiles and stretches his arms. I forgot what this is like. I think I was about to shrivel up and die.
Maddie: No doubt you have been low on energy. I've been waiting to see this a long time. So, what are you going to do about it?
Man: I'm going to tell her to get lost fast. I'm getting a woman who treats me right.

Maddie: Good for you, but I hope you take some time to be enjoy your freedom, even if it's uncomfortable. You deserve it.
Man: Yes, and now I understand. It makes sense, too. I'm going to go solo for a year before I look at another. I need time to get to know myself, then I'll shop around. Who knows? I may stay single a long time.
(They applaud as lights fade.)
Curtain.

Act IV

Scene 1: *In the same arrangement of chairs, Maddie, dressed in red, sits in front of a small group of men and women. The gold hat hangs on the rack beside her. A Caucasian man in his early forties speaks first.*

Man 1: I've tried every diet south of the Border and nothing works. The more I try to watch my weight, the more I gain. The last one I was on called Spinach Inches Off in Minutes, all it did was make me have to set up camp in the bathroom. That's a lot of crap. I don't know why I bother to come here.
Woman 1: I'm just fat and I can't help it. I don't have time to eat right. I have to work two jobs and grab something in between. Besides, it wouldn't matter. My mother is big and her mother was, so there's no hope. I'll never look like the women in that stupid book *Skinny Bitch*. I bet they are a mean bunch, too, from starving themselves all the time.
Man 2: My turn, huh? Okay. I'm a chef, so I love food and stay around it all the time. You could say I eat for a living and live for eating. So what am I doing here? I'm tired of being alone, and I like to have a girlfriend— maybe a family. I know I'm not healthy, so it's time.
Woman 2: Well, if I can't eat what I want, forget it! Life is too short not to have some pleasure. You never know when your time is coming. Besides, I love food. Everybody has got a weakness. At least it's not drugs or alcohol or porn.
Woman 3: Well, I guess I'm the odd ball. I wouldn't give a blind bat's bony butt about losing, but my doctor says I have to. I got heart trouble, and he says if I don't lose now, it'll rot off me underground. The old smartass! I ain't ready to down or up just yet.
(Smoke appears and the Fat Fiends dance on stage to slinky sounding music. One by one they speak.)
Beast of Bellies: I am Beast of Bellies, a stealthy, invisible thief. My job is delicious mischief— making you overeat. I never beg because I'm the mega-master of temptation. Making bigger bellies is my form of recreation. I lure you to fast food restaurants by telling big, fat lies that make you feed on greasy burgers and greasier French fries. My life on earth depends on making your tummies swell. What for me is wicked

pleasure is for you a living hell. (*He laughs and dances to the back as the next one comes forward.*)

Beelzebub of Bubble Butts: Pay no attention to baby beasty, who claims to have lots of guts. I'm the real scheming-demon, Beelzebub of Bubble Butts. I'm a fallen angel who used to do good deeds. Now I follow behind you to sew my wicked seeds. The wizard of deception, I make bottoms grow and flop like mushy masses of over-yeasted dough. I really get a thrill when you can't fit into a seat. As kids would say, my job is sweet! (*He dances to the back and the next fiend comes forward.*)

Sugar Booger: Did I hear someone call my name? Here I am to claim my fame. I'm such a sneaky, tasty tiny thing that everyone loves. They call me Sugar Booger. I come in an array of delectable disguises for every occasion that arises. I'm irresistible at birthday parties decorated, but I'm swallowed most when people don't think—like when they drink. Whether it's sodas or alcohol, they always swallow sugar-coated lies. Though I am tiny as grains of sand, I have gazillions of addicted fans! (*He dances to back and three others linked arm-in- arm dance forward.*)

Cellulighters: Hot from hell we come in endless droves making humans ugly from their heads to toes. Our lives depend on fat that makes us grow, so we do the ugly work we learned below. We can multiple as fast as swarms of flies. Our favorite places to habitate are butts and thighs. We're artists, of a sordid sort— your skin our clay. We sculpt you with lumps and streaks that look like sin. Oh. In case you haven't guessed, our name rhymes with *fighters*. It sounds phony but true to say we are Cellulighters. (*They giggle wickedly and move back as another one comes forward.*)

Thane of Thighs: I am the mighty Thane of Thighs, and I call my home Thunderland. I wander down thighways inch by inch, poking you with my wicked stick. I tickle and bite and make you wince, so you'll eat and eat until you're sick. My job is cushy unless some fools make up their minds to lose weight. Then I feed them subliminal thoughts until they overeat and become sedate. I'm Thane of Thighs, a blue blooded fiend; making you miserable makes me serene. (*He shakes his stick and dances to the back. The next one comes forward.*)

Troll of Triple Chins: Fold after fold after fold. What a sickly sight to behold! Layers of flabby skin that used to be a single chin. Beneath those triple folding rolls lives me—a wicked troll. A genius I am, indeed, at making you fulfill my needs. I have bags of gaudy- naughty tricks to make you eat until you're sick. There's nothing else I care to do but make a fat-faced fool out of you. I whisper sweet things in your ears, and you feed me desserts galore. How dear! Then I mutter a secret oath to make you stuff them in your mouth. I move slow and am always quiet unless you mention the bad word, diet! (*He whispers it and all the fiends cringe, gasp, and shake.*) Then I'm thrown into a panic, and they say I become quite manic. I know if you become too thin, I will lose and you would win. Then I would fail the ultimate test to drag your chin down to your chest. (*All Fat Fiends join hands and dance in a circle, chanting as they go off stage.*)

Fat Fiends: We're the mighty Fat Fiends, who follow wherever you go. Only one thing can stop us, and that you'll never know. (*The laugh as they run off stage. Ominous music plays. The men and women in the circle talk among themselves in amazement.*)

Man 1: Well, that explains everything!

Young girl: Fiends! You mean, like we're demon possessed?

Woman 1: Get behind me, Satan!

Maddie: Calm down, Friends. Not so fast. Didn't you hear what they said last? Only *one thing* can stop them. So let's figure out what it is. We have more power than those big bullies. I'll see you next time. Blackout.

Scene 2: *Lights out on group and slowly fade in to full bright. The Fat Fiends are scattered around behind them. From time to time they hover in a circle.*

Maddie: Here we are again and doing just as we agreed last month—fighting Fat Fiends. Let's hear some good news.

Woman 1: (*She gets the gold hat from the rack and puts it on*). I tell you I got madder and madder thinking about those devils, so I prayed and prayed and something came over me. I made up my mind to go to a gym for the first time in my life. Let me tell you there was this little man there, who thought he was a hot dog and I was a watermelon. Well, I got him straight fast. Here's what I said. And you say if I jiggle in place like this, I'll be glad in the long run because I'll be able to see something happen to me? Well, you better be right! I may look like a blubber-butt blown up; but I tell you, Brother, I can move, I say, move! I can get moved, be moved, move up, and move down. shake all this stuff around and move you over; mow you down like a bad weed. And furthermore, I can squeeze you until nothing's left but the sound where you thought you had been all this time. Now, you still want to shake me, Mister, or has my commotion taken all this running notion out of you? I mean, you ain't talking to no Miss-I-So-Nice- A-Sista-I-Twista-For-You-Mista-If-You-Get-Me-What-I-Want. Uh, Uh! You get me running and something better come out of this! You claim you can get these humps off my hips just like skinning an opossum. You got eyes wide enough to take me all in? I ain't no sugar baby— like where there's more meat, the more sweet. Uh-uh! All of this blubber, Buddy, is pure, and hands off! Anyhow, you don't look like no Sugar Daddy unless you really hiding something I can't even imagine on you, much less see. Don't get me wrong, here. I can run all right. Been doing that most years I can remember, and I ain't got where I was going yet. So this running in place (which sure ain't going no where) is one thing I can do, but I don't see how that's going to shrink any of me. Well, enough flapping your lips. Let's see you in action first. Lord have mercy on my giggling gizzard! Look at that pale turtle! He ain't even fanning the air, Move over, snail-face, and let Mama put this fat to flapping. If I ever get the notion to get into motion, ain't nothing can stop me. I could plow through a whole team of football fools and make flapjacks out of the leftovers. You just set there and call the pounds per mile. Right on for the treading for shedding, I call it! Look out for the jelly rolls! This mama is thinking shrinking! (*Applause from the group. One fat fiend slithers down in to the audience, up the aisle, finally exiting*).

Woman 1: In just a month I've lost inches and gained so much confidence I feel like a new person— bigger *inside* than out— at last! (*All laugh*)

Man 1: Well, good for you. Are you telling me praying did it? I don't believe a word of that stuff— tried religion years and years ago. It's all in your head.

Maddie: Friends, we're not here to argue about religion. How you understand life is different for everyone. As the saying goes,

"Whatever works!" What we want to focus on is what part we play in where we are and where we want to be. When you become aware, you will change.

Older woman: Well, I want to be alive for my new grandson. I decided I have something to live for more than myself, thank goodness. Now when I get ready to eat the wrong thing, I picture him, and feel a warm spot in my heart. Yes. I'm changing. (*Group freezes as lights fade on them and up on Wise Woman, who has been sitting in back row inside and unnoticed. She gets a gold hat from the rack and places it on the older woman's head.*)

Wise Woman: Let me tell you all about the fats (I said f-a-t-s) of life! Comes times in every life that strife and struggle and troubles do bubble up inside your head, but the danger comes in letting them spread on down to your feet in the fiercesome form of fat, which is your own sweet meat ballooning out of your skin 'till you feel like a constipated loon. You know you got this way from mess after mess that would test the patience of the best; so now you vow that tomorrow you'll diet, but meanwhile tonight's going be the big binge—the last time you'll take a bag of cookies or chips(why not both) to ease the pain of life's strains. Then comes tomorrow's sorrow and you find excuse for more self-abuse instead of seeking help for resolution of your persecution, which would lead to reduction in the production of the string of messes that's depressing you. Let's face the fat facts! You got a choice, Friends: either you keep on gaining weight— in which case you're losing ('cause this ain't no horse race), or you decide to swallow your pride and put a lid on your id and ego. Take something to bed that's either fast and full of action or slow and deep to put you to sleep. Hold on, and get your minds out of the pits! What I'm suggesting is a good book to feed your heart and head, so you get smart— not dead before your time. For the best way I know to get lean is to get serene.

Man 2: (*He jumps up and gets a hat from the rack and puts it on.*) I just felt it! I got it! I know my motivation, and it isn't even a woman— yet. (*They laugh*) I had a dream the night after first group. In it I had a new restaurant where I served only healthy dishes I created. It was so popular the lines of customers stood outside the door waiting. So I've been experimenting on recipes and eating them. I've lost a few pounds. It won't be long before my dream is a reality. When it is, I want to thank you all by inviting you for a free meal.

Young girl: *(She stands, and he hands her the hat she puts on.)* You all are such an inspiration. Last week I got accepted to graduate school, and I know I want to be fit. At the next meeting, you'll see a change. I feel it inside me now. It's like a rush of energy. I know I can!

Maddie: That's wonderful. Let's remember that this is a process and temptations will be around often. (*Fat Fiends slither around in the background. Two of them come forward*) Don't get discouraged. Keep faith to overcome anything.

Curtain

Act V

Scene 1: *Lights are dim as shadows move behind the veils. The man with the flashlight comes out from them. The first woman comes out and bumps into him.*

Man: I've been trying to find you. Are you okay?
Woman: I told you to leave me alone. What do you want? Money? You won't find any on me.
Man: No. I want to help you if you'll let me. That's the truth. I don't need money.
Woman: You wouldn't understand. I can't even explain. You can't do anything. It's just life. Haven't you noticed?
Man: I used to but not much any more. Please let me try to help. Just tell me what you are afraid of.
Woman: Easy. I'm tired of fighting everything day after day, year after year. What's it's all about? You never know what will happen next, which one will come after you. It's like being in a war and dodging bullets— only I don't know what I'm fighting for.
Man: A war with whom?
Woman: (*pointing to the shadows and people*). Are you blind? Them! (*As she names each thing, a shadow moves*) Murderers, spies, rapists, thieves, debt, war, drugs, accidents, diseases, con artists, scams.
Man: Ah, I see, but there is a way out. Believe me, I know, I used to be in there, too.
Woman: Yeah. Right! You were probably born rich. Well, I have to work hard for people who don't appreciate me— just to pay the bills, which I never can. They keep growing like mold or fungus. And that's just one of the problems. (*He stands still just looking at her. A man dressed in all black comes from the shadows. When the woman runs away from him, another appears and follows her. She runs and all freeze as Wise Woman appears.*)
WiseWoman: I'm telling you, AIDS disease ain't got nothing on fear, which has plagued us ever since that devil snake in the garden hissed the first lie to Eve, bless her heart. That's exactly where fear was born—right there in Eve's ear, which is why it is spelled *e-a-r* with an *f* stuck in the front. And as near as I can figure, that's where fear started

breeding in us like flies. Now the only way to remove this curse is to face it head-on, heart-fast like you are the boss-of-all-ages, the queen of I-mean-what-I-say-and-do, and I'm calling the bluff on your stuff. The lesson I am confessing for you here is that you got to face old fear head on, or it will ruin your life like a bad case of diarrhea. Use the brain God gave you as dominion over everything— be it man, woman, or beast. If you project good and reject fear, the bad tucks its tail and disappears until another Chicken Little comes squalling by. (*She exits stage right, and the woman is approached again by the men in black until she comes running towards the man who tried to help her. He takes her by the hand and leads her to the other end of the stage.*

Man: Will you let me show you now? You can't keep running all of your life. That's not the answer.

Woman: (*obviously exhausted*) But what can you do? I tried everything I know. As soon as I get rid of one, another one appears. Everybody wants something.

Man: Yes, I'm sure you have tried. So do you think you are just a victim of everybody and everything?

Woman: It seems that way most of the time.

Man: Are you willing to listen to me? I assure you I don't want any money. Will you give me a chance?

Woman: Okay. I'll listen.

Man: What is your worse problem right now?

Woman: I told you before. That's easy— money or rather debt! No matter how hard I work, there is never enough. Prices keep going up. I feel like I'm juggling in quicksand. Credit card interest and rent and gas go up but not my salary. Bills, bills, bills!

Man: What if I told you money is not the real problem. What if I say, and no disrespect intended, that you are blind?

Woman: Blind! Huh? Either you don't' understand or you are crazy. I see all too much. Everywhere I look people are having the same problem— except, of course, the ones getting rich off of us—like the politicians. There's no way to fight all of them. You must be blind! (*Men and women come forward with items—clothes, jewelry, shoes— to buy and signs advertising prices. As they approach the woman, she goes to each one trying things and obviously interested in buying.*)

Man: Yes. I used to be blinded by all of that. Let's look at *one* thing at a time. Do you know any ordinary people who may not be that rich but who are not overwhelmed with debt? You're seeing everything but through a hazy magnifying glass— not on purpose, of course.
Woman: So, mister, do I need glasses or Windex?
Man: Neither. You only need the one obvious but hard to find thing in the world.
Woman: That must be a winning lottery ticket.
Man: I doubt it. That would not solve your problem long. Most likely you would still have money problems. What I'm talking about works on everything and it lasts as long as you want it to.
Woman: I have no idea what you mean, but I'm ready to listen. You do seem sincere.
Man: I am, but are you? Are you ready to believe there might be a solution? You have to believe. It's easy, but it's an inside job.
Woman: Believe me! I am ready. There has to be something more to life than this. Wait a minute! I knew there was a catch. What do you mean by "an inside job"?
Man: (*grinning*) Bad choice of words, maybe. I mean you are bigger than your problems. Don't worry. I'm not talking about anything criminal. Just sit down and take a few deep breaths. (*He goes to the hat rack, gets a gold hat and places it on her head. Purple light shines on her. She gets up, smiles, and walks around. Veils lift between her and the frozen shadow people. She makes motions with her hands and they fall to their knees one at a time.*)
Woman: At last I see. I can handle my problems. (*The woman goes back to front to the man who helped her.*) Thank you! I feel like I have just awakened from a bad dream— a nightmare.
Man: (*smiling*) Indeed you did.
Woman: Thank you so much. I really like you now that I can really see you clearly.
Man: I like you, too. I felt it when I first saw you. That's why I've been trying to help you. (*They move closer and he takes her hand.*)
Woman: (*She grins at him*) We're mirrors now, aren't we?
Man: Yes. (*He kisses her gently on the cheek. as a shower of gold paper hats falls from the ceiling. Music: "A Hero Lives in You"*)

(The rest of the cast comes forward— all wearing gold hats. They are joined by Destiny and Wise Woman. The cast picks up gold hats one at a time and tosses them into the audience.)

The End

Glossary of African Terms Used In Part I "Women of Weya"

chenura–ceremony for the deceased's spirit
chikwambo–animal with magical powers that can avenge wrongdoing
Chimurenga– war of liberation
chipwa–ceremony to pray for rain
hanga–guinea fowl
hwahwa–beer
kufamba famba–to be promiscuous
kuoma rupandi–being paralysed
kutando botso–ritual to appease a relative's angry spirit
kuzisungirira–to hang oneself
lobola–bridepiece
mujibha–errand boy who assists in freedom fighters
mumvee–sausage tree with sweet juice fruit
mupfuhwira–love potion to make one's marriage partner love the giver
muroyi–witch
musosawafa – tree leaves used for washing after burying the dead
n'anga–traditional healer and diviner
ngozi–avenging spirit
nhanzva–soap brush; found in hills and mountains
ninga–cave
nyamukuta–midwife
povo–ordinary people, the masses
pungwe–political meetings held at night during a liberation war
rapoko – seed for beer
runyoka–charms to punish a man who commits adultery
upenyu–life
uroyi–witchcraft
vatengesi–sellouts, betrayers
zongororo – millipede

About the Author

Katherine De Lorraine holds an M.A. in English and M.F.A. in creative writing and has taught English and creative writing in colleges, universities, and secondary schools.
Publications credits include a prize-winning chapbook, numerous poems in journals and prizes in state poetry societies. De Lorraine is also the recipient of residency fellowships at Virginia Center for the Creative Arts. She lives in Roanoke, Virginia, where she writes, edits, advises, and teaches.
Website: www.movingwritealong.com

www.ingramcontent.com/pod-product-compliance
Lightning Source LLC
Chambersburg PA
CBHW051445290426
44109CB00016B/1677